THE
GREEN FACTORY

CREATING LEAN AND SUSTAINABLE MANUFACTURING

THE
GREEN FACTORY

CREATING LEAN AND SUSTAINABLE MANUFACTURING

Andrea Pampanelli • Neil Trivedi
Pauline Found

CRC Press
Taylor & Francis Group
Boca Raton London New York

CRC Press is an imprint of the
Taylor & Francis Group, an **informa** business

A PRODUCTIVITY PRESS BOOK

CRC Press
Taylor & Francis Group
6000 Broken Sound Parkway NW, Suite 300
Boca Raton, FL 33487-2742

© 2016 by Taylor & Francis Group, LLC
CRC Press is an imprint of Taylor & Francis Group, an Informa business

No claim to original U.S. Government works

Printed on acid-free paper
Version Date: 20150618

International Standard Book Number-13: 978-1-4987-0785-5 (Hardback)

Visit the Taylor & Francis Web site at
http://www.taylorandfrancis.com

and the CRC Press Web site at
http://www.crcpress.com

Contents

Foreword by John Bicheno

Steven Johnson, in *Where Good Ideas Come From*, described the "Adjacent Possible" as being a central way in which innovation has progressed. This approach takes good ideas from "adjacent" areas and modifies, adjusts, adapts, and integrates them so as to produce significant steps forward. Much of Lean and its precursors followed similar paths. Henry Ford took concepts from meat disassembly, division of labor, scientific work and work standards and, enabled by newly developed electric motors that increased quality and power, created the assembly line.

It was a logical step therefore that led Lean into "Lean is Green." Energy conservation has been the concern of mechanical engineers for decades. Perhaps Lean's entry into the area began with transport and reject wastes. Quick attempts focused on the modification of the seven classic wastes to include wasted energy, water, and materials. Predictably, the Green value stream concept began. Books and reports followed.

With the publication of *The Green Factory*, Andrea and her coauthors have pushed the boundaries even further. The book extends the "adjacent possible" of Lean and Green to develop the Lean and Green Business Model, taking as it does the best from "planet, people, and profit" and showing the application at cell, factory, and "extended product" areas. Of particular importance is the eminently practical guidance material on how to do Kaizen activities in such areas. Extending the already great value of the book, the authors have gone further to include key implementation lessons (different from standard Lean), and an extremely valuable section on preconditions for success.

Although it is based on Andrea's PhD studies, the book is not an academic treatise but an extended case study of implementing the Lean and Green Business Model in a major international company. This makes it uniquely valuable.

Andrea pursued her PhD research, and the application of the research, while an associate of Lean Enterprise Research Centre. It was my good fortune to meet her there. In her work, she was assisted by Neil, a full-time manager within her company, but also a graduate of the MSc Lean Operations program, and by Pauline as one of her PhD supervisors.

Alongside the meaty "how-to" material, Andrea's journey of Lean and Green discovery is described. Like several good innovations, this was not a linear path. Andrea, being Andrea, tells it like it is. That should be an encouragement to all who set out along the Lean and Green path. It is not a simple, straightforward journey and obstacles will be encountered—methodological, political, economic, and human. There remains much to learn, but this practical work will remain the standard reference for years to come.

John Bicheno
MSc Lean Enterprise Course Director
Buckingham Lean Enterprise Unit
University of Buckingham

Foreword by Robert W. "Doc" Hall

In this book, the authors add a great deal of experiential insight into a subject that should be attracting much more attention—the merging of Lean process improvement with environmental process improvement. Unfortunately, in most companies, a big gulf still separates Lean initiatives from environmental ones. Efforts by a few environmental practitioners to tag onto the surge in Lean programs in the United States have not gained much traction.

Much of this book details Andrea Pampanelli's experience with Lean and Green Kaizens in the Brazilian factories of GKN, a 256-year-old British manufacturing company with a bent toward environmental responsibility. As it is related, those projects not only improved the environment but also reduced GKN's costs. One reason for success was that GKN managers both understood and supported the projects. Lack of top management interest, or even awareness, is the bane of many improvement initiatives of both the Lean and the environmental kinds.

A strength of this book is that it characterizes failed and mediocre projects as well as the kind that proponents like to tout. The authors present no formulas; the book is not an engineering handbook; it's a managerial guide to Lean and Green improvement. However, the details of execution from a managerial view have value, so managers risk missing some key lessons if they don't dig into the details.

The authors note that compared with Green projects, improvement projects that eliminated environmental wastes by piggy backing on the improvement disciplines of Lean showed better results, including bottom line results. Lean improvement often concentrates only on value streams whereas environmental improvements must often address processes that feed multiple value streams. I have been personally frustrated by the separation of the Lean and the environmental communities. They have much to learn from each other. The authors' observations blaze a pathway leading forward in this collaboration.

This pathway is summarized in the 5-step "Lean and Green Business Model." For practitioners eager to avoid the pitfalls in the pathway, the authors also summarize seven prerequisites for implementing the five steps.

The prerequisite that struck me was #4: A supporting management team operating by leadership standard work and by Gemba leadership. Translated from Lean lingo, this means that senior leaders can't just bless a program and wish it to happen; they have to be involved, clearing picayune organizational system obstacles, authorizing resources, and demonstrating that they too are doing their part to make projects succeed. By coincidence, a big global survey crossed my desk a few days ago, and topping the list of reasons for Lean program failures was this same lack of leadership by senior managers.

A second finding, although not surprising, is very important. Information systems and data collection are crucial. In Lean improvements, we may improve process visibility without having much data—but the purpose of the visibility is to make hidden issues more obvious. One cannot know how well improvements are progressing without having a baseline of measurement from which to compare. This is even more crucial for environmental wastes. Unless waste is gross, electricity use, water consumption, toxic releases, and volatiles in the air escape notice. We don't fix what we don't see.

A general methodology for Green improvement is the same as for Lean. Set a standard; stabilize. Improve the process; set a new standard and restabilize, meaning that all details and support needed to hold the standard are worked out. And make the process visible so that deviations from standard and "sore spots" stick out. Problems get attention when they can't be put out of mind.

The model sets a baseline of general knowledge about how to do this. I hope that you enjoy the book, and more than that, that you are inspired to do Lean and Green yourself, in your factories. A glimmer of a dream is that practitioners into Lean and Green will form a group to share their experiences and learn from each other. That has worked well in many places for Lean practitioners, and everyone is better off for it. It should continue to work well when the scope of improvement is enlarged.

Robert. W. "Doc" Hall
Professor Emeritus
Indiana University
Bloomington, Indiana

Chairman
Compression Institute
Hondo, Texas

Prologue: A New Way of Thinking

We cannot solve our problems with the same thinking we used when we created them.

But in real life, how many times have you tried to see the same problems using different ideas, applying different lenses, trying to understand different paradigms, applying different ways of thinking?

Systems thinking is the process of understanding how things, regarded as systems, influence one another within a whole. As a culture, we are discovering that we cannot understand the major problems of our time in isolation. These are systemic problems; they are by nature interconnected and interdependent. In this sense, systems thinking means thinking in context. It is a way of thinking that emphasizes the whole rather than the parts. While classical science insists that the behavior of a complex system can be best analyzed in terms of the properties of the parts, systems thinking reverses the equation by showing that the properties of the parts are not intrinsic but can be understood only within the context of the larger whole.

According to Capra (1996), an understanding of reality based on the essential interdependence and interconnectedness at the heart of things restores our human connection to the entire web of life. Living systems exhibit the same basic principles of organization. They are networks that are organizationally closed, but open to the flows of energy and resources. Their structures are determined by their histories of structural changes and they are intelligent because of the cognitive dimensions inherent in the processes of life. In business terms, the interchange of ideas and concepts exists even though there is no real intention for them to occur.

Rooted in systems thinking, sustainability grounds the development debate in a global framework, within which a continuous satisfaction of human needs constitute the ultimate goal (World Commission on Environment and Development, 1987). When transposing this idea to the business level, corporate sustainability can accordingly be defined as meeting the needs of a firm's direct and indirect stakeholders (such as shareholders, employees, clients, pressure groups, communities, etc.), without compromising its ability to meet the needs of future stakeholders as well. Toward this goal, firms have to maintain and expand their economic, social, and environmental capital base while actively contributing to the sustainability in the political domain. From this definition, three key elements of corporate sustainability can be identified: integrating the economic, ecological, and social aspects in a "triple bottom line."

In this sense, human well-being and progress toward sustainable development are vitally dependent upon improving the management of Earth's ecosystems to ensure their conservation and sustainable use. But while demands for ecosystem services such as food and clean water are growing, human actions are at the same time diminishing the capability of many ecosystems to meet these demands. Sound policy and management interventions can often reverse ecosystem degradation and enhance the contributions of ecosystems to human well-being, but knowing when and how to intervene requires substantial understanding of the characteristics of the systems involved in a holistic way, including the ecological or environmental aspects, the social systems involved, and the business or economic issues.

What happens when we try to solve this problem looking at sustainable principles inside a manufacturing business operation? From the 1980s, many models of "how to run" an efficient and effective manufacturing organization have been developed. This process was to yield a new and post-mass production model of manufacturing that has been termed "Lean production" and more recently "Lean thinking." The origins of the "Lean approach" can be traced to U.S. fears in the 1970s that newly emerging Japanese assemblers held a competitive advantage over their established Western counterparts. Those fears promoted benchmarking studies of the global automotive industry to test these fears and find the causes of such an advantage. The publication, *The Machine that Changed the World* (Womack et al., 1990), reported the results of this study. A follow-on book titled *Lean Thinking* (Womack and Jones, 1996) established the five Lean principles upon which a "more efficient" manufacturing business, viewed through the lens of quality, delivery, and cost, can be based. For the last 25 years, companies have tried to establish their business models based on these principles of establishing what customers value, creating streams of value-adding product or services that flow at the pull of the demand from the customer, while striving for perfection.

Einstein also stated:

> Learn from yesterday, live for today, hope for tomorrow. The important thing is never stop questioning.

This period in which we live is marked by increasingly frequent and intense encounters of all kinds, with a global trend toward mixing and hybridization (Burke, 2006). Understanding that there are different ways to be sustainable in a manufacturing business, the intention of this book is to integrate two different ways of thinking: Lean thinking and Green thinking.

We know that walls, or organizational structure, cannot stop the flow of ideas but it does not mean that they are able to flow through so easily. Lean and Green thinking are rooted in different ways, have different meanings, and occupy different spaces inside the business world. The idea of this book is to see both ways of thinking and, based on different perspectives, understand its own characteristics, boundaries, and languages, yet be able to explain each one to each other and to create an integrated approach, applying important characteristics from both of them. The Kaizen events will be the moment where these two different ways of thinking meet. The Japanese word for "improvement," or "change for the better," Kaizen refers to a philosophy or practices that focus upon continuous improvement of processes. When used in the business sense and applied to the workplace, Kaizen refers to activities that continually improve all functions, and this involves all employees, from the CEO to the assembly line workers.

Therefore, the main objective of this book is to propose a new model, the Lean and Green Business Model (L&GBM), where the Green dimension, the environmental aspect of sustainability, is added to the pure Lean thinking concept in order to create a new way of thinking that contributes to and balances the three sustainability dimensions (people, profit, and planet) and one that uses a Kaizen approach for dealing with and improving mass and energy flows in a manufacturing environment that already possesses a deployment level in applying Lean. The model aims to have the following characteristics:

1. Lean thinking for dealing with manufacturing environmental issues in order to integrate environmental sustainable practices prerequisites of (1) impact reduction and (2) resources productivity with manufacturing ways of working

2. The use of the Kaizen approach for dealing with and improving environmental flows of mass and energy of a manufacturing cell and the value stream

3. The idea of improving operational sustainability by optimizing supporting flows performance—the mass and energy flows (everything that enters and leaves) of systems composed by a production for a cell and a value stream

Figure P.1 presents the main part of the study.
As Einstein once said,

> No problem can be solved with the same level of consciousness that created it.

This book proposes a new framework, a model, that is able to translate the environmental language and the intention of the environmental sustainable practices of pollution prevention, improvement of environmental performance, improvement of mass and energy flows to the manufacturing world. In other words, it means looking at environmental issues with manufacturing eyes, in another way, and by understanding existing manufacturing practices and tools, adapting it based on environmental fundamentals and using it to support a sustainable business. L&GBM aims to translate the environmental language to the manufacturing world, through applying Lean thinking.

Along with the development of L&GBM, this book also describes the journey of implementing a new framework in global corporation.

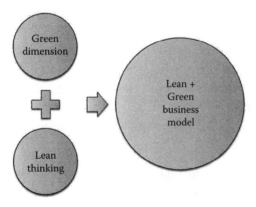

FIGURE P.1
The main objective of the study. (From Pampanelli, A., *L&GBM*, PhD thesis, School of Engineering, UFRGS, 2013.)

Therefore, this is the story of developing and implementing L&GBM in GKN, a major British multinational company with operations in more than 30 countries, more than 140 manufacturing businesses, and employing more than 50,000 people around the world. Founded in 1759 in South Wales, United Kingdom, GKN was one of the first companies to bring the modern industrial age to life. Today, after more than 250 years, this global British engineering company produces special systems and structures, with a focus on automotive, powder metallurgy, aerospace, and land systems markets.

GKN is a major first tier supplier to the automotive and aerospace industries with established solid foundations and policies in both Lean and environmental fields. In the Brazilian driveline plant this story is based upon, a strong focus on environmental improvement projects had been in place since the year 2000, with more than 83 environmental research and development projects established between 2000 and 2010, resulting in a 99% recycling rate, but also with significant further opportunities identified to reduce the environmental impact of the business.

Lean was introduced in 2004 in the GKN automotive sector to improve competiveness in that market and one of the early significant milestones was the support by senior leadership for the Site Continuous Improvement Leader (SCIL) training program. This series of training workshops took promising manufacturing leaders and trained them to expert level over a period of a year. These leaders returned to their home sites and became the local Lean change agents for their factories focusing on the deployment of Lean to manufacturing processes. This structure became the backbone of Lean deployment at GKN.

This book investigates the next stage for GKN in becoming a sustainable manufacturer with the integration of Lean and the concepts of sustainability, Lean and Green, by developing a model (L&GBM) that can be applied to manufacturing. By using Lean thinking to solve environmental problems, L&GBM will be focused on the improvement of the manufacturing supporting flows (water, energy, material, effluent, chemicals, and wastes) with the ultimate goal of optimizing the overall process performance by reducing costs and significant environmental impacts. Further, in order to create the basis for the L&GBM deployment, this book explores some of the fundamental building blocks of operations management, Lean thinking, sustainability, and Green concepts. It proposes the model structure and dynamics and reports the application of the developed model in a major engineering international corporation. The results of the applications are presented, analyzed, and conclusions are proposed.

BUSINESS CHALLENGES THAT LEAD TO LEAN AND GREEN

In a classic Lean deployment, one of the ways to initiate the system is through a value stream map that identifies the key wastes and impediments to flow. The teams seek to eliminate the classic seven wastes and improve the flow of value for the product. Once this cycle has been completed, the same pattern follows across the factory while smaller incremental improvements are made in the original value stream through the deployment of continuous improvement systems. The efforts are focused on getting the improvements to stick and setting up methods to check-act the different elements of deployment.

Once these systems are mature, the question "where to next" can simply arise or perhaps the team cannot see any further opportunities to unlock efficiency. They may be limited in their paradigm by sticking to the seven wastes and not considering them in a wider context to encompass mass and energy inputs and wastes. The introduction of Green thinking to this mindset can stimulate a whole new avenue of efficiency. A simple example of one site we visited who thought they had "done Lean" identified that they left most of their machines running when there was no product. They gained immediate savings by switching them off when idle.

Lean has many entry points, but one of the negative points is that it has often been (mis)associated with cost reduction. At one site visited, there was a high degree of hostility to Lean as it had been used in the past to cut costs. However, introducing Green thinking to the group stimulated a high degree of motivation and they subsequently identified numerous environmental savings. They felt they were doing something for the environment rather than the company—which they resented for a number of reasons. It could be argued that using Lean and Green will be the new entry point for Lean.

One of the sustainment questions that occurs during the mature phase of deployment is how to keep the stimulus for new ideas and engagement. One way is to introduce new environmental parameters to consider and provide a new stimulus to the improvements.

Manufacturing organizations are under continual pressure to reduce costs. Although Lean can provide a step change in performance, Lean is now commonplace in many manufacturing organizations. So the question is how can they differentiate further their product? Adding Green credentials not only reduces costs but also enhances their public image.

One aspect, which can drive Lean and Green thinking, is the noncompliance to environmental legislation. This can often be caused by a failure of plant, equipment, or excessive scrap and/or poor disposal. While many of these can be resolved by direct intervention and a spot fix, the introduction of Lean thinking into this arena allows for a more comprehensive systematic approach to solving the problem.

In the large organization we operated in, similar to other manufacturing organizations, there was a clear boundary between manufacturing and other functions. Manufacturing typically being the dominant function in terms of size and responsibility took the lead on what initiatives it would deploy and what it would support. Clearly traditional Lean is well within these functional boundaries; however, consideration for environmental improvements was often seen as compliance-led rather than efficiency-led and hence not embraced as comprehensively as Lean.

Although there was specific training for nonmanufacturing functions in Lean, this focused on the office and accidentally excluded most of the EHS managers. Although attempts were made to create a training workshop for this group, it never materialized. As a consequence, the environment, health and safety (EHS) managers were on the periphery of the site-based change process through a lack of knowledge of how the Lean system worked. The EHS managers therefore struggled to get a foothold in the factory cycle of improvement and change and used compliance as a way of increasing pressure for environmental change. Bringing together Lean and Green broke down these organizational barriers and enabled a conduit for environmental thinking to enter the factory.

When the environmental deployment background is considered, a number of issues and challenges are identified. Figure P.2 presents some of the challenges faced.

In GKN, there were a number of factors that came together to suggest that the deployment of environmental thinking was not fully integrated into the business. Although included in the business excellence assessment criteria, environmental deployment was seen only on the periphery of the core of operations and perceived as a legislative necessity rather than a commercial advantage. The original main focus of change and the improvements for factories was the changes generated through traditional and Lean thinking that could be made to operations to generate savings or improve efficiency. The direct benefits of environmental deployment to the business were not fully understood and therefore not fully integrated within the organization and operations.

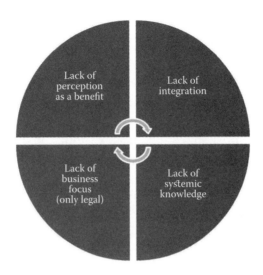

FIGURE P.2

Challenges faced by the environmental function. (Developed by the authors.)

In terms of the people and organization, roles were often left vacant or combined with other roles that made it impossible to develop the expertise or consistency for the environmental roles. This resulted in physical and knowledge gaps that generated an overall lack of competence in environmental deployment. Implementation was therefore driven more through compliance rather than structured strategic deployment.

In order to be successful in environmental implementation, the organization has to recognize that it is a true benefit to business operations. It not only has to be part of the strategy but also deployed effectively and checked for system effectiveness. There has to be recognition of the skills and competencies required to deliver this aspect of the business model and acceptance that it is another form of change improvement. As with other forms of change, delivery needs to include a wider range of people, the typical diagonal slice through the organization covering different functions and management levels. This breadth of people will uncover the issues and problems that need to be solved across the entity. Figure P.3 shows this concept.

This book seeks to answer the following questions:

1. Can Green thinking be applied in the factory using Lean techniques?
2. Is there a benefit using this method?
3. Are there tangible improvements as a result?

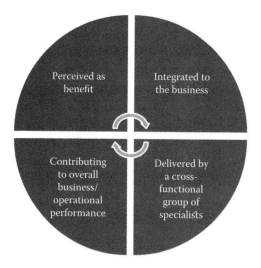

FIGURE P.3
The potential benefits of the environmental function within the organizations. (Developed by the authors.)

The book is titled *The Green Factory* to illustrate that the factory system has to be considered a whole entity for Green thinking to be fully effective. If only part of the factory is subject to "Green," that is, by focusing only on one cell or department, a natural paradox will exist between the different cells or departments within a value stream with a risk that gains in specific cells will fall back to their original condition over time.

The deployment must encompass the whole factory as many mass and energy flows are not typically measured by machine and so have to be apportioned from a total level to the value streams/cells to get meaningful data.

1

Introduction to the Lean and Green Business Model

CONCEPT BEHIND THE MODEL

Sustainability has become a legacy for the twenty-first century. It embodies the promise of societal evolution toward a more equitable and richer world in which the natural environment is preserved for generations to come. The quest for economic growth and social equity has become a major goal for most of the past 150 years. By adding concern for the carrying capacity of natural systems, sustainability ties together the current main challenges facing humanity.

Although the issues embodying sustainability are more than a century old, the concept of sustainable development itself was described in the late 1980s, following The Brundtland Report, a report made by the World Commission on Environment and Development. It describes the growing global awareness of the enormous environmental problems facing the planet, and proposes a growing shift toward global environmental action. The concern about the sustainability encouraged the society to support the development of a significant number of corporate practice, many applied to manufacturing business, such as industrial ecology, industrial symbiosis, pollution prevention, cleaner production, etc., with the ultimate goal of supporting the sustainability dimensions of (1) profit, (2) people, and (3) planet. Although all these studies and practices have contributed to create a new world paradigm, very few were able to contribute fully to all dimensions of sustainability (Lozano, 2012).

Sustainable development links the concern for the carrying capacity of natural systems with the social challenges facing humanity. It contains two key concepts:

1. *The concept of needs*, in particular the essential needs of the world's poor, to whom overriding priority should be given
2. *The idea of limitations*, imposed by the state of technology and social organization on the environment's ability to meet present and future needs

All these definitions of sustainable development propose understanding the world as a system—a system that connects space and time. The concept of sustainable development is rooted in systems thinking.

Systems' thinking is based on the belief that the component parts of a system can be best understood in the context of relationships with each other and with other systems, rather than in isolation. It is the process of understanding how things, regarded as systems, influence one another within a whole. It is an approach to problem solving, by viewing "problems" as parts of an overall system, rather than reacting to specific part, outcomes or events and potentially contributing to further development of unintended consequences (Capra, 1996).

"…manufacturing is the constant game of doing more with less…" therefore manufacturing managers are constantly looking for new approaches to increase efficiency (Hopp and Spearman, 2008). With the purpose of promoting a continuous improvement culture within the business, the expenditure of resources for any goal, other than the creation of value for the end customer, is considered to be wasteful. Lean thinking is one of these strategies that are being explored by manufacturing to increase performance. The logic of Lean thinking can be redesigned and integrated to the sustainability systemic concept.

"…a gram of prevention is better than a kilogram of cure…;" therefore, using less energy, material, generating less waste is prevention, and very good for the environment (Baas, 2007). Minimizing the waste produced in manufacturing, reducing energy use, and using materials and resources in a more efficient way can lead to financial cost savings and a reduction of environmental impacts. Therefore, integrating both concepts, Lean thinking and sustainability, offers the foundation for a new business logic, where the pillars of sustainability, social, economic, and environmental, can be better understood by manufacturing and therefore support business goals, requirements, and needs.

Thus, in a systems approach, there are no such things as "physics problems," "economics problems," "production problems," etc., the way a part affects the whole depends on other parts. To improve the performance of a system, you have to improve the interactions, not just the parts. Also, most managers attempt to solve the problem that they recognize. That is the fundamental reason why most management interventions fail. In fact, most problems are best solved outside of the system. The 'disciplines' (physics, engineering, sociology, marketing, economics, etc.) are simply points of view, ways of looking at problems. "Lean" is but one way. Most system problems are intertwined. Often, benefits result by looking at the system in a different way.

Following this, the main objective of this book is to propose a new model, the Lean and Green Business Model (L&GBM), where the Green dimension, the environmental aspect of sustainability, is added to the pure Lean thinking concept, in order to create a new way of thinking that contributes and balances the three sustainability dimensions (people, profit, and planet). Lean takes the Kaizen (continuous improvement) approach for dealing and improving mass and energy flows in a manufacturing environment that already possesses a deployment level in applying Lean.

Taking a systems' thinking approach involves an understanding of a system by examining the linkages and interactions between the elements that compose the entirety of the system. Considering this, the basis for this book is rooted in four main pillars: understanding about "operations management," the main principles that make manufacturing behave the way it is; "Lean thinking," and why it changed manufacturing ways of working; "sustainability" and the triple bottom line of profit, people, and planet; and "Green thinking," how it is integrated to the manufacturing world. The intersection between these main knowledge streams, as presented in Figure 1.1, provides the foundation for the development of the L&GBM.

In science, systems thinkers consider that a system is a set of interrelated parts functioning as a whole to achieve a common purpose, a dynamic and complex whole, interacting as a structured functional unit. Therefore, subsystems are interdependent. A change in one part affects other parts. The whole is greater than the sum of its parts.

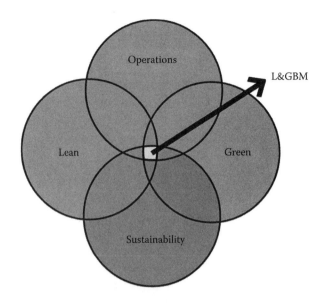

FIGURE 1.1
The main pillars for the concept behind this book. (From Pampanelli, A., L&GBM, PhD Thesis, School of Engineering, UFRGS, Porto Alegre, Brazil, 2013.)

The individual bodies of literature are subsystems that compose the L&GBM, which are interrelated, interdependent, and synergic. The understanding of the individual bodies that is the basis to compose the L&GBM, is key to create the structured functional unit of this book.

INPUTS FROM OPERATIONS MANAGEMENT

According to Hopp and Spearman (2008), operations management is a function within the organization responsible for the flow of material through a plant and for getting product out the door. Therefore, the role of operations management is strategic. Designing the way that manufacturing will be developed is a core task in this process.

The operations view focuses on the flow of material through a plant and thereby places clear emphasis on most of the key measures by which manufacturing managers are evaluated (throughput, customer service, quality, cost, investments, labor cost, and efficiency). Adopting an operations viewpoint in the design process therefore promotes design for manufacturability. Operations and strategic planning are closely tied, since strategic decisions determine the number and types of products to be produced, the size of manufacturing facilities, the degree of vertical integration, etc.

Slack et al. (2004) contend that the main purpose of operations management, the part it plays within the organization, is strategic. For the authors, the reason that the functions exist is based on three roles: to implement business strategy (put it into practice), to support business strategy (by developing resources to provide the capabilities within the organization to improve and refine strategic goals), and to drive business strategy (by giving long-term advantage).

Manufacturing may be designed in a variety of different ways and approaches. This book develops an understanding of the differences and characteristics of either a Lean or a Green manufacturing operation and presents a model that combines these to give a Lean and Green business that addresses the three pillars of sustainability—economic (profit dimension), social (people dimension), and environmental (planet dimension).

POWER OF LEAN PRODUCTION

The concept of Lean thinking describes the working philosophy and practices of Japanese vehicle manufacturers and in particular the Toyota Production System (TPS). In TPS, the use of a resource that is not viewed as a value by the client should be a candidate for elimination. In general terms, Lean thinking is defined and described by five key principles (Womack and Jones, 1996):

- *Specific value*: Define value precisely from the perspective of the end customer in terms of the specific product with specific capabilities offered at a specific time.
- *Identify value streams*: Identify the entire value stream for each product or product family and eliminate waste.
- *Make value flow*: Make the remaining value-creating steps flow.
- *Let the customer pull value*: Design and provide what the customer wants only when the customer wants it.
- *Pursue perfection:* Strive for perfection by continually removing successive layers of waste as they are uncovered.

One of the key aspects of Lean thinking is simplification (Pettersen, 2009; Karim and Zaman, 2013). Expanded to the context of the whole process, or plant, it gains the wider ability to save simultaneously resources and space, materials, energy, transportation, and time. Considering economic principles, Ohno (1988) describes seven classic wastes in the context of manufacturing processes. They are overproduction, waiting, transport, overprocessing, inventory, motion, and defects.

Resource productivity and closed-loops provide better services, for longer periods, with less material, cost and hassle. The logic of Lean thinking, with the emphasis on eliminating seven classic wastes, makes customer-defined value flow continuously with the aim of producing less waste. Together, these practices offer the foundation for powerful new business logic. Instead of simply selling the customer a product, it is perceived appropriate to derive what is desired, considering quantity, rate, and manner. Based on the analysis of customer value, Lean presents a set of tools and techniques for continuous improvement processes and eliminating wastes (Rother and Shook, 2003).

The essence of Lean thinking lies in people involvement (Bhasin and Burcher, 2006; Pollitt, 2006). Kaizen (Japanese word meaning continuous improvement) provides the employees a platform to unleash their creativity. Dr. J. Edward Deming was the pioneer in this field, developing in the 1950s what was called the *Deming*, or *Shewart*, *Cycle*, a simple and effective technique that serves as a practical tool to carry out continuous improvement in the workplace. This technique, also called the PDCA (plan, do, check, and act) cycle, provides conceptual as well as practical framework, while carrying out Kaizen activities by the employees. According to Womack and Jones (1996), the key building block of Lean thinking is Kaizen—a process-oriented philosophy with a focus on incremental improvements and the standardization of the improved system as the building block for further improvement. Kaizen philosophy has two major objectives (Berger, 1997; Saurin and Ferreira, 2009):

- *Develop a problem-solving culture:* with focus on analysis and problem solving by applying scientific and structured thinking. Lean philosophy presents a variety of tools and techniques with the ultimate goal of improving processes and eliminating wastes. Developing a problem-solving culture is key for deploying Lean thinking (Berger, 1997);

- *People involvement:* Kaizen relies on ongoing effort and engagement of people—it is based on the constant effort for involving and integrating people, from shop-floor workers to senior executives. The key for successful Lean thinking is based on the capacity for training and involving everyone. Based on this idea, people systems are considered more successful than software systems for sustaining the results. This creates a learning environment, with long-term maintenance of results and openness for creativity and improvements (Berger, 1997).

Four Dimensions of a Lean Enterprise

Bicheno (2000) states that the general purpose of Lean thinking can be described in four main dimensions: (1) safety, (2) quality, (3) delivery, and (4) cost. It means that, "producing exactly what the customer wants, exactly when (with no delay), at fair price and minimum waste" is the ultimate goal of a Lean enterprise. Therefore, Lean thinking focuses on the optimization of production resources oriented by the customer—time, people, machine, space, etc.—and consequently reduces wastes.

Table 1.1 expands on these four dimensions by linking them to the objectives of stability, control, and competitive advantage.

The logic of implementing Lean needs to be considered as it will be used to gain consensus throughout the entire organization. This follows the objectives in Table 1.1, which Rich defines as a roadmap from chaos to competitive advantage. The first step is to stabilize the process and ensure a safe environment in which people can work where basic discipline is established and morale is high. The next step is to improve quality as no Lean enterprise can exist with poor quality; as the quality improves, costs will come down and the ability to deliver on-time will improve. It is only when this system is in control should the focus move to cost improvement, first in the supply chain and then in the design (Rich, 2006). Figure 1.2 describes the Lean improvement stages from chaos to control to competitive advantage.

While every Lean journey is unique, there are certain features of the model that are common to all Lean implementation models. The "house of Lean " concept is often used to present the natural order of the common features of a system and operational change process to implement Lean production (Figure 1.3). This model suggests that Lean production can only be achieved when it is put together correctly

TABLE 1.1

Four Dimensions of a Lean Enterprise

Dimension	Key Objective	Description
Dimension 1: Safety	Stability	No world-class business exists in an environment with poor safety standards and morale. It is difficult to get the best from people if the factory is a mess and the basic organization is not in place. If the factory is disorganized, it is difficult to tell the difference between good and bad standards of professional conduct. It also means that it is difficult to see the value from waste and the danger that exists in even the simplest of working environments. It is a basic right to expect that the factory is safe, even though it may not be world class or Lean.
Dimension 2: Quality		The second stage in the logic of Lean implementation is to address the quality of everything that is done in the factory. It means understanding the value of doing what you do and how to do it better to provide higher levels of value. This stage, just like the first, is designed to create stability from the chaos. It means also that the organization has implemented a problem-solving structure, the basis of TQM. Improving quality improves productivity and reduces the time needed to convert product and hence it lowers costs. A Lean production system follows this "quality first" route since increasing quality improves customer value.
Dimension 3: Delivery	Control	The third stage of Lean logic is delivery. If quality is good and constant, then products should flow better and therefore batch sizes and inventories can be reduced to allow quality products to be delivered in less time. Improving the delivery performance at each stage of production shortens the time between receiving and dispatching product orders. This stage involves the attention to "delivery issues" and the introduction of solutions that compress the time between getting the order and getting paid for it.

(*Continued*)

TABLE 1.1 (*Continued*)

Four Dimensions of a Lean Enterprise

Dimension	Key Objective	Description
Dimension 4: Cost	Competitive advantage	Stage four is where the issue of cost can be addressed effectively. With a high level of quality and delivery performance from the production system, what remains is to find ways to reduce unnecessary costs. At this point, wastes and cost become visible as "abnormal" parts of the production systems. All too often, this stage of improvement involves the questioning of policies around manufacturing processes and has not been questioned since the system was designed. Therefore cost reductions can take place and further waste eliminated from the production system that was not detected during the previous stages.

Source: Adapted from Rich, N., Understanding the Lean journey, in N. Rich, N. Bateman, A. Esain, L. Massey, and D. Samuel, eds., *Evolution of Lean: Lessons from the Workplace*, Cambridge University Press, Cambridge, U.K., 2006, pp. 11–31.

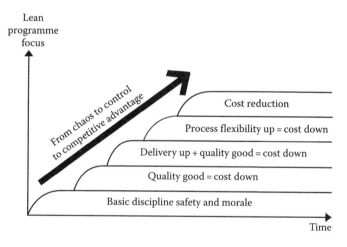

FIGURE 1.2

Lean improvement stages. (From Rich, N., Understanding the Lean journey, in N. Rich, N. Bateman, A. Esain, L. Massey, and D. Samuel, eds., *Evolution of Lean: Lessons from the Workplace*, Cambridge University Press, Cambridge, U.K., 2006, pp. 11–31.)

and when key organizational processes are brought together to give it strength. The foundations of the "house of Lean " are basic operations disciplines, the floor consists of simple and visual techniques as control mechanisms, the walls are produced from quality control, maintenance, and material flow pillars, joined by a culture of continuous improvement,

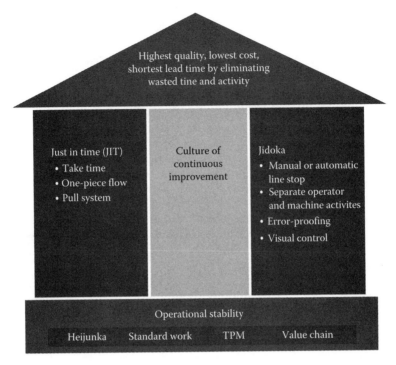

FIGURE 1.3
House of Lean. (Adapted from Rich, N., Understanding the Lean journey, in N. Rich, N. Bateman, A. Esain, L. Massey, and D. Samuel, eds., *Evolution of Lean: Lessons from the Workplace*, Cambridge University Press, Cambridge, U.K., 2006, pp. 11–31.)

which provide structure and robustness to the system. Finally, to keep everything synchronized and in place, there are the binding measures of the business and the use of factory policy settings to focus and give direction to the many improvement programs of the factory. It is not enough to have one piece or fragment; the power of Lean systems lies in the design of the total "system."

Building Lean manufacturing capability incrementally will, if exploited correctly, give local benefits, but until the basic Lean systems of quality and delivery performance are mastered, there will not be a great deal to offer the customer. For example—halving the set up time for a machine in the production process is actually meaningless, until the same savings can be achieved throughout the entire system; when output has increased throughout or boxes of unnecessary inventory are removed. To the companies that do not understand the logic, there has been little gain from the customer perspective. Instead, the company has made a "point improvement" in the manufacturing system, but this has been completely lost, as overall stocks have not been reduced.

Lean thinking is described as a "more efficient" manufacturing business based on the same manufacturing dimensions, the same original lenses of safety, quality delivery, and cost. However, a more systemic view of what was really necessary for shifting a mind-set was not taken into consideration. It derives from the fact that most of us, and especially our large social institutions, subscribe to the concepts of an outdated worldview, a perception of reality inadequate for dealing with our overpopulated, globally interconnected world.

SUSTAINABLE DEVELOPMENT AND "GREEN" THINKING

Humanity has always depended on the services provided by the biosphere and its ecosystems. Furthermore, the biosphere is itself the product of life on Earth. The composition of the atmosphere and soil, the cycling of elements through air and waterways, and many other ecological assets are all the result of living processes—and all are maintained and replenished by living ecosystems. The human species, while buffered against environmental immediacies by culture and technology, is ultimately fully dependent on the flow of ecosystem services. In this context, the sustainability concept was created.

Sustainability is a systemic concept relating to the continuity of economic, social, and environmental aspects of human society. It is however part of a wider and evolving field of corporate social and environmental responsibility, which in modern times has its roots in Rachel Carson's *Silent Spring* (Carson, 2010) and the Club of Rome's *The Limits to Growth* analysis (Meadows et al., 1972). The term was first used by the Brundtland Commission that coined what has become the most often-quoted definition of sustainable development; one that "meets the needs of the present without compromising the ability of future generations to meet their own needs" (Stern, 2007; Mazur and Miles, 2010).

The field of sustainable development can be conceptually broken into three constituent parts: environmental sustainability, economic sustainability and socio-political sustainability. Figure 1.4 presents a representative scheme of sustainable development vectors.

FIGURE 1.4
Sustainable development vectors. (Developed by the authors.)

The overall idea behind the Green thinking concept is the understanding of nature as something limited. Lozano (2008), in his article "Envisioning sustainability three-dimensionally," reviews the concept of environmental sustainability established by several authors and states that the Green thinking can be quoted as "use of natural resources without going beyond the carrying capacities and the production of pollutants without passing the biodegradation limits of the receiving system."

Therefore, the general purpose of Green thinking can be described in one dimension (Environment), with two main focuses (Moreira et al., 2010): (1) Producing with the maximum productivity in the use of natural resources and with the (2) minimum environmental impact. A Green company acts (or claims to act) in a way that minimizes damage to the environment. To this end, a Green company can apply different types of environmental practices. The Lean and Green Report (Zokaei et al., 2010) and the studies of Glavic and Lukman (2007) and Lozano (2012) provide an overview of several of these practices.

Three key examples of well-known environmental practices (also known as Green practices) include (1) cleaner production, (2) eco-efficiency, and (3) life cycle analysis (LCA). For Cagno et al. (2005) and Tanimoto et al. (2008), cleaner production is a preventive, company-specific environmental protection initiative. It is intended to minimize waste and emissions and to maximize productive output. By analyzing the flow of materials and energy in a company, source reduction strategies can be developed for minimizing waste and emissions in industrial processes. Improvements in organization and technology may help to reduce resource use or may suggest better choices in the use of materials and energy. These actions may lead to waste avoidance, including waste water generation, gaseous emissions, and waste heat and noise. According to Korhone (2007), eco-efficiency focuses on enhancing production while using fewer resources, which thus results in less waste and pollution. Seven critical factors are considered in eco-efficiency, including a reduction in the material intensity of goods and services, a reduction in energy intensity, a reduction in toxic dispersion, an enhancement of material recyclability, the maximum sustainable use of resources, a reduction in material persistence in nature and an increased service intensity of products. Finally, Haes (1993) notes that LCA models the complex interaction between a product and the environment from cradle to cradle, providing in-depth data on environmental impacts. LCA can be useful to manufacturing companies because it can show which activities, processes, and materials lead to particularly large environmental impacts, which can in turn serve as targets for improvement.

A number of mechanisms have been proposed by which companies can assess, monitor, and record the environmental impacts of their products, processes, and other activities and verify that plans to reduce impacts will be effective. In general terms, Green thinking practices can be generalized by four common key principles:

1. Identify environmental aspects and impacts
2. Measure environmental impact and the use of natural resources
3. Identify alternatives to (1) impact reduction and (2) resources productivity
4. Continuous improvement

Over the past decades, many different Green practices were created proposing the coexistence of the industry, the business, the people, the natural environment, and their interactions, such as Eco-Design and Design for Environment (Diehl and Brezet, 2004), Life cycle analysis, (Haes, 1993), Cleaner Production (Cagno et al., 2005; Tanimoto et al., 2008), Environmental Management Systems (Rondinelli and Vastag, 2000), and Environmental Performance Evaluation (Jasch, 2000). An overview and the main essence these five environmental sustainable practices are presented in Table 1.2.

TABLE 1.2

Overview of Key Strategies to Achieve Sustainability

Practice	Concept	Key Principles
1—Eco-Design and design for environment (DFE)	It is based on the principle of designing physical objects and services to comply with the principles of economic, social, and ecological sustainability in all stages of product or service development with the ultimate goal of reducing environmental impact in the whole product or service life cycle. While the practical application varies among disciplines, the seven more common principles applied to eco-design are as follows (Diehl and Brezet, 2004): Product dematerialization; product functional optimization; reduction in the number of parts and materials; production and transport optimization; materials selection and design; reduction of product usage impact; increase in product life cycle.	1. Design with environmental focus—reduction in the number of parts and materials 2. Selection of low impact materials 3. Reduction usage impact—increase product life cycle
2—Life cycle analysis (LCA)	LCA models the complex interaction between a product and the environment from cradle to cradle. LCA can be an expensive and lengthy process but provides in-depth data on the environmental impacts. It can be useful to manufacturing companies because it can show which activities, processes, and materials are creating particularly large environmental impacts, so that these can be targeted for improvement. The process has two main steps: (1) the inventory step, where the life cycle of the product or service is described and the raw material usage and emissions at each stage is recorded, and (2) the impact assessment stage, where data is accessed to understand how much impact of what type is associated with the emissions and material usage (Haes, 1993; Moraes et al., 2010).	1. Mass and energy inventory 2. Impact assessment

(Continued)

TABLE 1.2 (*Continued*)

Overview of Key Strategies to Achieve Sustainability

Practice	Concept	Key Principles
3—Cleaner production	Cleaner production is a preventive, company-specific environmental protection initiative. It is intended to minimize waste and emissions and maximize product output. By analyzing the flow of materials and energy in a company, one tries to identify options to minimize waste and emissions out of industrial processes through source reduction strategies. Improvements of organization and technology help to reduce or suggest better choices in use of materials and energy, and to avoid waste, waste water generation, and gaseous emissions, and also waste heat and noise. Examples for cleaner production options are presented below (Cagno et al., 2005): Documentation of consumption (as a basic analysis of material and energy flows); use of indicators and controlling (to identify losses from poor planning, poor education and training, mistakes); substitution of raw materials and auxiliary materials (especially renewable materials and energy); increase the life time of auxiliary materials and process liquids (by avoiding drag in, drag out, contamination); improved control and automatization; reuse of waste (internal or external); low waste processes and technologies	1. Process data collection 2. Define metrics—key performance indicators 3. Pollution prevention 4. Focus on the 3 Rs: reduce, reuse, recycle

(*Continued*)

TABLE 1.2 (Continued)

Overview of Key Strategies to Achieve Sustainability

Practice	Concept	Key Principles
4—Environmental management systems (EMS)	An EMS is a structured framework for managing an organization's significant environmental impact. The standard for EMS is ISO 14001, which is based on Deming's cycle of plan, do, check, and act. Companies are required to assess their main environmental impacts, and then plan to reduce them. Elements of the EMS include workforce involvement and continuous improvement and also measuring, recording, and auditing impacts and the efforts to reduce them. ISO 14000, the International Organization for Standardization's guidelines for environmental management systems, has become the international benchmark by which corporations can voluntarily develop and assess their environmental practices (Rondinelli and Vastag, 2000; Nawrocka et al., 2009; Gavronski et al., 2013). It offers a format for developing an environmental policy; identifying environmental aspects, defining objectives and targets, implementing a program to attain a company's goals, monitoring and measuring effectiveness, correcting deficiencies and problems, and reviewing management systems to promote continuous improvement. The main objectives of this standard is to support organizations in minimizing operations environment negative effect (that cause adverse changes to air, water, or land) and complying with applicable laws and regulations (ISO14001:2004).	1. Pollution prevention 2. Accomplishment of legal requirements 3. Continuous improvement
5—Environmental performance evaluation (EPE)	EPE is a management technique that allows evaluation of a company's environmental performance through self-defined criteria and requirements. The consequent data evaluation provides substantial information to the EMS, permitting the development and tracking of application-specific measurable objectives, goals, and strategies. EPE is a highly adaptable technique, which allows the creation of customized models. This concept has been described in the ISO 14031:2000 standard (Jasch, 2000).	1. Define metrics—key performance indicators 2. Data collection 3. Continuous improvement

Source: Pampanelli, A., L&GBM, PhD Thesis, School of Engineering, UFRGS, Porto Alegre, Brazil, 2013.

CONNECTING THE CONCEPTS: OPERATIONS, LEAN, GREEN, AND SUSTAINABILITY

Considering operations management characteristics as well as Lean thinking, sustainability and Green thinking, Table 1.3 presents the fundamental building blocks from the literature and describes the intersection between the main knowledge streams, which provided the foundation for the development of the L&GBM.

HOW LEAN AND GREEN THINKING CAN BE COMBINED INTO ONE CONCEPTUAL BUSINESS MODEL

The previous sections "Concept behind the Model," "Inputs from Operations Management," "Power of Lean Production," and "Sustainable Development and 'Green' Thinking" explored the main characteristics, dimensions, and fundamental building blocks of the main bodies of literature that compose this book. The objective of this section is analyzing the gaps and interactions between the individual blocks of literature that compose this work to establish the basis for the L&GBM. Within the text, eight hypotheses will be discussed and analyzed:

1. Lean practices require a higher level of integration with manufacturing integration than Green practices.
2. Green practices should consider a higher level of integration with manufacturing ways in order to achieve better results.
3. Most sustainability/Green practices do not fully contribute to the three core sustainability dimensions.
4. Pure Lean thinking contributes to two sustainability dimensions—(1) profit and (2) people.
5. Although they can support business improvement and strategy (such as reducing costs), environmental practices are often stated to be environmental protection initiatives.
6. There are several examples proving the synergy between Lean and Green practices but none has proposed a different way of thinking.

TABLE 1.3

Fundamental building blocks that compose operations management, Lean thinking, sustainability and Green thinking

	Operations Management	Lean Thinking	Sustainability	Green Thinking
What is it?	Function within the organization responsible for the flow of material through a plant and for developing whatever it takes to get product out the door.	A model of "how to run" an efficient and effective manufacturing organization.	Systemic concept relating to the continuity of economic, social and environmental aspects of human society.	Series of mechanism or practices created to better using natural resources or reducing of environmental impact.
Purpose	Support, implement, and drive business strategy.	"Producing exactly what the customer wants, exactly when (with no delay), at fair price and minimum waste." (Bicheno, 2000)	"Meets the needs of the present without compromising the ability of future generations to meet their own needs." (World Commission on Environment and Development, 1987)	"Use of natural resources without going beyond the carrying capacities and the production of pollutants without passing the biodegradation limits of the receiving system." (Lozano, 2008)
Dimensions	1. Quality 2. Delivery 3. Cost	1. Safety 2. Quality 3. Delivery 4. Cost	1. Social 2. Economic 3. Environment	1. Environment
Main principles	NA	1. Specific value 2. Identify value streams	NA	1. Identify environmental aspects and impacts 2. Measure environmental impact and the use of natural resources

(Continued)

TABLE 1.3 (*Continued*)

Fundamental building blocks that compose operations management, Lean thinking, sustainability and Green thinking

	Operations Management	Lean Thinking	Sustainability	Green Thinking
		3. Make value flow 4. Let the customer pull value 5. Pursue perfection		3. Identify alternatives to (a) impact reduction and (b) resources productivity 4. Continuous improvement
Examples of working tools	Six sigma Industrial engineering tools	Lean thinking tools Kaizen Problem solving People involvement	Industrial ecology Industrial symbiosis Eco-efficiency Eco-effectiveness Triple bottom line Natural capitalism The natural step The biosphere rule	Eco-design design for environment (DFE) Life cycle analysis (LCA) Cleaner production EMS EPE

Source: Pampanelli, A., L&GBM, PhD Thesis, School of Engineering, UFRGS, Porto Alegre, Brazil, 2013.

7. The application of pure Lean promotes environmental improvement even though there is no direct intention to reduce environmental impact.
8. A new way of thinking can be created by integrating to the pure Lean thinking one new dimension—(3) the planet.

Figure 1.5 presents a schematic representation of what will be reviewed in this section.

Analysis of Lean and Green through Operations Lenses

Although manufacturing may be designed in a variety of different ways and approaches, the first thing that is important to highlight is that taking a Lean or a Green manufacturing approach is a strategic organizational

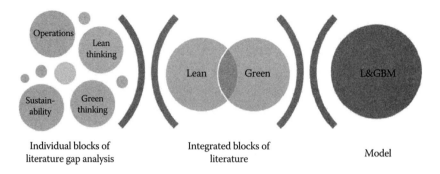

Individual blocks of literature gap analysis   Integrated blocks of literature   Model

FIGURE 1.5

Schematic representation of literature analysis. (From Pampanelli, A., L&GBM, PhD Thesis, School of Engineering, UFRGS, Porto Alegre, Brazil, 2013.)

decision, since this will drive the behavior and the process of the whole organization. Both Lean and Green manufacturing are interested in the way waste is handled. However, waste has different meanings in Lean manufacturing compared to Green manufacturing (Verrier et al., 2014).

Lean manufacturing perceives waste as non-value adding to the customer (Bicheno, 2000). Wastes in this case are overproduction, waiting, transport, extra processing, inventory, motion, and defects. A Lean manufacturing company is one that considers the expenditure of resources for any goal other than the creation of value for the end customer to be wasteful, which thus becomes a target for elimination (Womack and Jones, 1996). For reducing Lean wastes, it is important to understand the way that manufacturing occurs and its ways of working. To achieve this, a Lean enterprise is supposed to not only apply the five Lean principles but also integrate tools that assist in improving quality and identifying and eliminating waste. Examples of such "tools" are value stream mapping, 5S, Kanban (pull systems), and poka-yoke (error-proofing) (Bicheno, 2000). As waste is eliminated and quality improves, production time and costs are reduced. Essentially, Lean manufacturing is centered on preserving, or enhancing, value with less work.

On the other hand, Green manufacturing focuses on the environment and perceives waste as the extraction and the disposal of resources at rates or in forms beyond that which nature can absorb (Lozano, 2008). In other words, environmental waste is unnecessary, or excessive, use of resources or substances released to the air, water, or land that could harm human health or the environment (United States Environmental Protection Agency (EPA), 2006). Environmental wastes in this case are based on the mass and energy flow of the manufacturing processes, everything that enters and leaves the system. Environmental waste can occur when a company uses resources to provide products or services to customers and/or when customers use and dispose of products (EPA, 2006). For reducing environmental wastes, it is important to understand in detail the mass and energy flows of the manufacturing processes, what is used, how much, where it comes from, what is generated after production, and how the left-overs from production will be treated. A Green manufacturing company acts (or claims to act) in a way that minimizes the impact to the environment. To this end, a Green company can apply different types of environmental practices. The overall objective of such environmental practices is to (1) improve the productivity in the use of natural resources, such as energy and materials, and (2) reduce environmental impact (Moreira et al., 2010).

Although Lean and Green manufacturing can both be considered strategies to run and to improve manufacturing, they have distinct characteristics (Diaz-Elsayad, 2013). The difference here is not just the waste concept already explored, but the focus and the level of integration both need to have with the manufacturing processes prior to implementation. If one intends to be Lean and to apply Lean working tools, it is necessary to develop a deep understanding and integration with all manufacturing processes. In contrast, the environmental improvement may occur by focusing on the manufacturing mass and energy flows without needing a deep understanding of the manufacturing processes and procedures. Therefore, Lean manufacturing touches the heart of the manufacturing processes, although Green manufacturing may exist without this level of integration.

This situation highlights an important characteristic that drives distinct behaviors in implementing Lean and Green tools. While the application of a Lean manufacturing tool to reduce waste and to improve production flow requires deep changes in the manufacturing ways of working (machines, process, people, and materials), the implementation of an environmental tool, to reduce environmental wastes, may happen with a focus only on in the improvement of mass and energy flows, sometimes leaving out of this process, not only manufacturing ways of working, but also machines, process, and people. Therefore, since it does not present a systematic approach for dealing with all manufacturing variables, in many situations Green manufacturing improvements are considered something that is "nice to have" as long as "real manufacturing" is done.

This idea may partially explain a question asked by Kiperstok (2000) when reviewing a well-known Green practice, cleaner production. In the article, the author starts by asking the following question: "If cleaner production practice so obviously makes common sense, why do they not occur naturally in industry?" Lack of integration may be the answer here. Jabbour et al. (2012) developed a study regarding EMS deployment in Brazil. According to the authors, environmental management can be considered a new competitive manufacturing priority in companies located in Brazil, capable of influencing the manufacturing dimensions of cost, quality, flexibility, and delivery. A study of 63 companies suggests that Green thinking needs to be integrated to other functional areas in order to succeed and deliver a competitive advantage.

The success of Lean thinking in solving manufacturing problems, in integrating with manufacturing variables, and in understanding the manufacturing characteristics (Saurin and Ferreira, 2009; Yang et al., 2011) shows an important characteristic to be taken into consideration in order to Green practices to succeed in terms of being accepted and considered as part of manufacturing world: To succeed in manufacturing, the strategy needs to be completely integrated to the manufacturing ways of working and variables (Jabbour et al., 2012). Otherwise no long-term survival can be guaranteed.

Analysis of Lean and Green Taking a Sustainability Perspective

Sustainability is the capacity to endure. For human beings, sustainability is the potential for long-term maintenance of well-being, which has ecological, economic, political and cultural dimensions (Schrettle et al., 2013). The difficulty in making the sustainability concept and its application clear has been explored by many researchers to understand the concept more deeply. Glavic and Lukman (2007) present a study that summarizes the definition of sustainability and its terms. Lozano (2008) identifies the need for many to fully understand the concept, presenting a study that not only expands the concept of sustainability but also clarifies its dimensions. The same author in a second study (Lozano, 2012) presents research that discusses how a company's voluntary sustainability initiatives contribute to the sustainability dimensions.

Table 1.4, adapted from Lozano's study, presents a list of these sustainability/Green strategies (most of which also explored by the Lean and Green Report (Zokaei et al., 2010)) and how they contribute to the sustainability

TABLE 1.4

Examples of Sustainability/Corporate Strategies and Their Contribution to the
Sustainability Dimensions

Sustainability/ Corporate Strategies	Sustainability Dimensions		
	Profit/Economic	Planet/ Environment	People/Social
Sustainable livelihoods	**Full contribution**	**Full contribution**	**Full contribution**
Triple bottom line	**Full contribution**	**Full contribution**	**Full contribution**
The natural step	Partial contribution	**Full contribution**	Partial contribution
Environmental management system	None	**Full contribution**	None
Environmental and social accounting	**Full contribution**	**Full contribution**	**Full contribution**
Life cycle analysis	None	**Full contribution**	None
Cleaner production	**Full Contribution**	**Full contribution**	None
Design for environment	None	**Full contribution**	None
Eco-efficiency	**Full Contribution**	**Full contribution**	None
Industrial ecology	**Full Contribution**	**Full contribution**	None
Factor X	Partial contribution	**Full contribution**	None
Green chemistry	None	**Full contribution**	None
Corporate social responsibility	None	Partial contribution	**Full contribution**
Sustainable reporting	**Full contribution**	Partial contribution	Partial contribution
Corporate citizenship	None	None	**Full contribution**

Source: Lozano, R., *J. Clean. Prod.*, 25, 14–26, 2012.

three-core dimensions of (1) economic, (2) environment, and (3) social.
With different structure and priorities, all these strategies describe conditions for sustainable systems and propose strategies in order to make the sustainable development concept viable.

The conclusion drawn from Table 1.4 is that, although these concepts are 20 years old, most of those sustainability/Green strategies have their main focus on environmental conservation. The majority, as they are proposed, is not integrated, or part of, the fundamental building blocks of the manufacturing strategies.

Therefore, following that idea, it is possible to conclude that there is a lack of sustainability/Green strategies capable of contributing to the core three dimensions of sustainability (people, profit, and planet) that are fully integrated to the main aspects of the business. Although sustainability is a systemic concept, proposing the integration of environmental issues with social and economic aspects of the society, balancing our transaction activities in order to reflect natural systems, the most popular environmental sustainable practices are not able to cope with the three sustainability dimensions.

As discussed previously, Bicheno (2000) argues that the general purpose of Lean thinking can be described in four main dimensions (1) S-Safety, (2) Q-Quality, (3) D-Delivery, and (4) C-Cost. It means that "producing exactly what the customer wants, exactly when (with no delay), at fair price and minimum waste" is the ultimate goal of a Lean enterprise. Therefore, Lean thinking focuses on the optimization of production resources oriented by the customer—time, people, machine, space, etc.—and consequently reduces wastes.

Hines et al. (2004) suggest that pure Lean thinking not only focuses on one dimension of sustainability, (1) profit, but also supports another, (2) the people. Considering scientific methods and involvement of people as basis for its tools, and technique, Lean presents a robust methodology for incorporating the social, people, dimension in a systems thinking approach. Therefore, according to the authors, pure Lean thinking contributes to two dimensions of the sustainability concept:

- Fully contributes to the "profit dimension" due to its core focus on eliminating the seven classic wastes and reducing costs
- Partially contributes to the "people dimension" due to its focus on the "Kaizen" continuous improvement philosophy for solving problems and involving people

Hawken et al. (1999) discuss that there is a great potential for integrating Lean thinking with environmental sustainability. Lean created a new manufacturing paradigm, which includes an environmental sustainability element. Therefore, Lean thinking is Green when it also considers the reduction of materials and energy that are required by the production as well as the wastes produced by production. Until recently, Lean manufacturing and the application of Lean thinking has concentrated on the economic and some of the social aspects of sustainability. However, the essence of Lean is to produce more with less, this implies that Lean thinking organizations use less resource, in regards with raw materials and energy.

Hall (2010) argues that although Lean thinking already explores some aspects of sustainability, people, and profit, sustainability goes beyond, including the idea of environmental impact—mass and energy flow of everything that enters and leaves the system. Therefore, based on a Lean thinking approach, to manage the three core sustainability dimensions (people, profit and planet), a Lean manufacturing business has to focus on eliminating wastes (profit) and "Kaizen" (people), and also to explain the movement of mass and energy within, and through, boundaries, even if these boundaries are only a production cell, the entire factory, or the supply chain (planet).

Analysis of Green Taking a Lean Perspective

The general idea behind the Green thinking concept is the understanding of nature as something limited. The general purpose of Green thinking can be described in one dimension (environment), with two main foci (Moreira et al., 2010): (1) Producing with the maximum productivity in the use of natural resources and with the (2) minimum environmental impact.

Although the idea of Lean thinking has not been extensively explored by environmental practitioners, many articles have referred to Lean thinking fundamentals, such as the need for people involvement (Venselaar, 1995; Boyle, 1999; Remmen and Lorentzen, 2000; Stone, 2000; Perron et al., 2006), learning by doing (Dieleman and Huisingh, 2006), continuous improvement (Fresner, 1998), and problem-solving tools (Calia et al., 2009). These principles have been used in studies that apply environmental practices to show that there is a connection between Lean and Green practices. Lean tools and fundamentals are successful when used for promoting environmental improvements.

To the researchers that recognize the existence of Lean thinking, there have been several initiatives discussing positive and negative aspects of using Lean to support the environment, using different aspects and tools of Lean for solving environmental problems.

Hawken et al. (1999) have discussed that there is a great potential for integrating Lean thinking with Green thinking. Since the essence of Lean is to produce more with less, this idea implies that Lean thinking organizations use less resource, that is, raw materials and energy.

Gustashaw and Hall (2008) state that in an organization in which Lean is already the heart of its business system and Kaizen is the basis for the continuous improvement culture, the same strategy could be expanded to improving production energy and material flows. Deploying a strategy of improving the way that products and materials are sourced, manufactured, marketed, and disposed of at the end of its life cycle means that Lean thinking can be used for creating a sustainable manufacturing. The authors state that, by Lean logic, or thermodynamic environmental improvement of mass-energy balances, the holistic improvement within a factory system boundary can greatly benefit an existing business model. There are few practices or models (Kurdve et al., 2011) that integrate Lean thinking and Green thinking and merge its fundamental principles.

Hajmohammad et al. (2013) in a study comparing Lean and Green practices concluded that environmental practices are the main driver for reaching better environmental performance. Therefore, integration is key. A model that connects a Lean thinking approach to Green business practices is also supported by pure Green practices.

Therefore, while researchers have explored the idea of an integrated approach, no one has fully explored the potential of adapting Lean thinking to establish a new model for pollution prevention. Nevertheless, existing research supports the following conclusions:

- The main objectives of environmental practices are (1) improving the use of natural resources and (2) reducing the environmental impact. Although these can support business improvement and strategy (such as reducing costs), environmental practices are often stated to be environmental protection initiatives.
- There are few practices or models (Kurdve et al., 2011) that integrate Lean thinking and Green thinking and merge its fundamental principles (for Lean manufacturing, the five key principles; for Green manufacturing, (1) improving the use of natural resources and (2) reducing environmental impacts) to create an integrated model that considers and prioritizes Lean and Green manufacturing simultaneously.
- There is no environmental practice that considers a certain level of manufacturing stability, or Lean deployment, as a prerequisite.

Analysis of Lean Taking a Green Perspective

Lean sees waste as anything that is non-value adding to the customer (Bicheno, 2000). On the other hand, *Green* sees waste as extraction and consequential disposal of resources at rates, or in forms, beyond that which nature can absorb (Lozano, 2008). An environmental waste is an unnecessary, or excessive, use of resources or substances released to the air, water, or land that could harm human health or the environment (EPA, 2006). Environmental waste can occur when the company uses resources to provide products or services to customers and/or when the customers use and dispose products (EPA, 2006).

A concern of many businesses was that improving environmental performance may undermine the economic sustainability of an organization and that they could not afford the cost of meeting their environmental responsibilities. However, there are many examples in which improving environmental performance has improved a company's profit. Moreover, several authors have identified that Lean manufacturing has had a significant contribution to the environment (Maxwell et al., 1993; Porter and Van Der Linde, 1995; King and Lenox, 2001; Cobert and Klassen, 2006).

Several studies analyzing synergies between pure Lean thinking and environmental improvement practices discuss the positive and negative aspects of using Lean manufacturing to support environmental practices. These studies apply different aspects and tools of Lean manufacturing to solve environmental problems and therefore contribute to more sustainable business.

Vais et al. (2006) published a study entitled "Lean and Green" that considers a Romanian secondary tissue paper and board mill. They analyzed the development of technical environmental projects aimed at accomplishing legal requirements and the use of Lean tools, such as 5S, the Kaizen philosophy, and autonomous maintenance; these tools were used to develop incremental improvements, which in turn optimized the use of natural resources and production output.

EPA published *The Lean and Environmental Toolkit* in December 2006 (EPA, 2006) to demonstrate that traditional Lean tools can be applied to environmental waste. This manual established guidelines for using Lean manufacturing tools to improve material flow among the main flows that support the production process and that in turn can affect the environment (such as energy, chemicals, and other kinds of waste). Some of the key findings reported by EPA are as follows: (1) Lean produces an operational and cultural environment that is highly conductive to waste minimization and pollution prevention. (2) Lean can be leveraged to produce even more environmental improvement. (3) Some regulatory "friction" can be encountered when applying Lean to environmentally sensitive processes. (4) Environmental agencies have a window of opportunity—while companies are embarking on Lean initiatives and investments—to collaborate with Lean promoters to further improve the environmental benefits associated with Lean.

Biggs (2009) studied the integration of Lean thinking and environmental improvement and concluded that the Lean approach can help to make the case for environmental impact reduction to businesses. This is because Lean thinking is capable of providing environmental benefits, even though there is no direct intention to reduce environmental impact, and moreover, Lean thinking can be used to make environmental improvements as well as productivity improvements.

Biggs' (2009) conclusion supports those of Womack and Jones (1996), who maintained that Lean thinking principles can help make Green practices more effective by exposing hidden Green waste and eliminating it. The highlights of some of the authors' findings are as follows:

- Lean, as it is, is capable of providing environmental benefits even though there is no direct intention to reduce environmental impact. Reduction of Lean wastes has effects in reducing environmental impacts.
- The application of Lean tools, such as reduction of inventory (Kanban), Just in Time, Right first time, Kaizen, Standard Work, 5S, mapping, and problem solving can contribute to reducing environmental impact.
- The Lean methodology can be used to make environmental improvements as well as productivity improvements.
- Kaizen/continuous improvement (CI), Kaizen blitz, and workforce involvement and suggestions are popularly suggested methods of gaining environmental benefit from a Lean implementation.
- It is the culture of waste elimination and experimentation, problem solving, and improvement of best practice encouraged by Lean that may help companies to make environmental improvements.
- A Lean approach can help to make the business case for environmental impact reduction.

Moreira et al. (2010) developed a study integrating the concepts of Lean thinking and eco-efficiency. After analyzing several publications that explore the relationship between Lean and Green manufacturing, the authors identified the three main causes of production waste due to weak environmental performance: (1) energy consumption, (2) material consumption, and (3) pollutant emissions. The authors developed a framework for integrating the seven classic Lean wastes (i.e., overproduction, inventory, transportation, motion, defects, waiting, and overprocessing) with previous types of environmental impacts, energy use, materials consumption, and emissions and they showed that environmental waste is embedded within the seven classic production wastes. Although the authors do not explicitly outline the main characteristics of Lean thinking, this study supports the notion that Lean thinking can help make the case for environmental impact reduction to businesses.

Salleh et al. (2012) integrated information management in environmental management systems practices with TQM (total quality management) in Lean manufacturing. The goal was to achieve total communication efficiency using a Green and Lean TQM system. This system manages information while also addressing environmental concerns. Their study provides some preliminary insights, especially for companies looking for a suitable system to improve their productivity through efficient information management. This study further proves that Lean and Green information systems can be integrated and that the same database can support both systems.

In more recent research, Dues et al. (2012) discussed how Lean practices can act as catalysts for Greening operations. The authors suggest that the Lean and Green connection goes beyond the notion of waste reduction and in fact overlaps in areas such as (1) tools and practices, (2) supply chain relationship, (3) lead time reduction, (4) the focus on people and organization, and (5) the use of techniques for waste reduction. The applied literature analysis developed by the authors identified that Lean manufacturing not only serves as a catalyst but also is synergetic for Green manufacturing. Their research findings include the following:

- Green practices are no longer optional for companies and cannot be ignored. A Green company is not necessarily a Lean company, as Lean thinking is focused on manufacturing efficiency. Additionally, by introducing Green practices into a Lean operating environment, companies will often have to make trade-offs between multiple objectives that are not perfectly compatible.
- Lean manufacturers, however, are often Greener than nonlean companies. Green manufacturing is a natural extension to Lean manufacturing, although many Lean practices are Green without the explicit intention of being Green.
- Lean manufacturing can serve as a catalyst to facilitate the implementation of environmental improvements. Lean thinking

processes are beneficial to Green practices, and the implementation of Green practices has a positive influence on existing business practices.

- The integration of Lean and Green practices benefits companies. The hesitation toward Green practices is fuelled by the fact that there is confusion about Green manufacturing, and there are very few independent models, regulations, and best practices that support its implementation. Because Green practices are not the focal point of many companies, the potential to maximize Green gains with the implementation of a simple Green framework is significant. Therefore, it is essential to integrate both strategies and implement these simultaneously to fully exploit the synergetic effect.

Over the last two decades the Lean community has focused on the operational aspects for continuous improvement, but these studies demonstrate that there are intrinsic linkages between Lean and Green—not least due to the relentless focus of Lean on waste elimination. In the Lean model, work is based on the principles of continuous improvement, or "Kaizen." Workers are responsible for identifying quality problems found on the production line and, in contrast to mass production, are able to stop the line for such problems. Shop-floor workers are arranged in teams, with a team leader performing a coordinating role in addition to assembly tasks (Rothenberg, 2001). A benefit of pollution prevention activities is that they are often "value-added" for the firm since they reduce costs through reduction in material use or through the avoidance of waste management costs (Florida, 1996; Found, 2009).

The next challenge for the Lean community is to consciously account for the environmental issues. Gordon (2001) discusses some ways for integrating Lean and Green practices with a focus on cost reduction practices. In the fundamental text, *Natural Capitalism*, Hawken et al. (1999) discuss the importance of not only developing a more sustainable society, but also of how different existing practices can be applied to support an environmentally oriented business.

Gavronski et al. (2012) highlight the effect that a plant-level social climate has on fostering a greater emphasis on pollution prevention. Managers, in order to promote pollution prevention should promote both social climate and knowledge exchange in the plant. Managers should also support environmental management systems, not as a bureaucratic process of documentation and regulatory compliance, but as a source of process improvement and innovation. As discussed, the fundamental building block of Lean thinking is continuous improvement, Kaizen, with its focus on problem solving and employee involvement, which fits perfectly with the notion of creating a Greener industry. Therefore, the pursuit of continuous improvement, creates substantial opportunities for pollution prevention and waste and emissions reduction.

Understanding the Connections

This section has presented the analysis of the gaps and interactions of the individual blocks of literature that compose this book to establish the basis for the L&GBM.

Following the analysis presented here, it is possible to highlight the fundamental ideas identified in the literature, which are presented in Figure 1.6.

From these conclusions, the inputs and analysis will be the basis for proposing a new model, named the Lean Business & Green Model (L&GBM), whereby environmental sustainability is integrated into the pure Lean thinking concept. The model adopts a Kaizen approach to

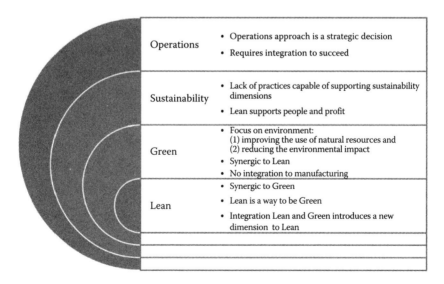

FIGURE 1.6
Fundamental ideas identified in the literature analysis. (From Pampanelli, A., L&GBM, PhD Thesis, School of Engineering, UFRGS, Porto Alegre, Brazil, 2013.)

address and improve mass and energy flows in a manufacturing environment that already possesses a sufficient deployment level in applying Lean manufacturing.

The model was designed to be applicable at the cell and value stream levels through cross-functional Kaizen team events that ensure that all team members are fully involved and have the opportunity to contribute their ideas.

2

Lean and Green Business Model and Operational Implementation

L&GBM

In science, systems thinkers consider that a system is a set of interrelated parts that function as a whole to achieve a common purpose, a dynamic and complex whole, interacting as a structured functional unit. Therefore, subsystems are interdependent, meaning that a change in one part affects the other parts and the whole is greater than the sum of its parts. The individual bodies of literature are subsystems that compose the Lean and Green business model (L&GBM), which are interrelated, interdependent, and synergistic (Galeazzo et al., 2014). Its individual understanding is the basis to compose the L&GBM, the structured functional unit of this research.

Therefore, Chapter 1 explored the main characteristics, dimensions, fundamental building blocks, and main tools of the four main bodies of literature that compose this study:

1. Operations management
2. Lean thinking
3. Sustainability
4. Green thinking

This understanding is key for building and creating a new model. Chapter 1 also proposed an analysis of gaps and interactions of the individual blocks of literature that compose this work to establish the basis for the L&GBM.

Analysis of the literature highlights the following ten conclusions, which are fundamentally important for the design of the L&GBM:

1. Being Lean or Green is a strategic company decision.
2. Taking Lean manufacturing approach requires higher level of integration with manufacturing processes than Green manufacturing. Green practices that want to succeed in terms of improving manufacturing should consider a higher level of integration with manufacturing ways of working and variables.
3. There is currently no environmental practice that considers a certain level of manufacturing stability, integration, or Lean deployment as a prerequisite prior to be implemented.
4. Green practices have basically two main objectives: (i) improving the use of natural resources and (ii) reducing the environmental impact.
5. Most Green/sustainability practices do not fully contribute to the three sustainability dimensions. Pure Lean contributes to two sustainability dimensions: (1) profit and (2) people.
6. Lean helps a company to become Green, even if there is no direct intention to reduce environmental impact. A company's adoption of Lean manufacturing can be the first stage in becoming Green.
7. There are intrinsic linkages between Lean and environmental practices. Studies prove synergy between Lean fundamentals while applying Green practices. Lean tools and fundamentals are successful when used for promoting environmental improvements.
8. The full integration of Lean and Green practices with fundamental strategic objectives should benefit companies.
9. There are few practices or models (EPA, 2006) that identify and measure environmental aspects and impacts based on manufacturing value streams.
10. Integrating Lean and Green may introduce a new dimension to the traditional Lean thinking model.

This section of the book is dedicated to explaining the design and fundamental characteristics of the L&GBM, a model that aims to translate the environmental language to the manufacturing world, applying Lean thinking to solve environmental problems. Therefore, this chapter presents the purpose, the principles, and the ways of working of the L&GBM, as well as the explanation why it is different from pure Lean and pure Green.

It also illustrates how the new model was applied across different manufacturing environments and explores in detail how the engagement of the relevant stakeholders was key to the success of the project. The L&GBM model is described as it was applied in real life by the authors in their factories. The initial Kaizens were held on carefully chosen sites, which had a high level of successfully deployed and sustained Lean culture. As a result, the pilot projects begin to expose the value that can be generated by taking this approach through the results that were achieved. The pilots also provided the evidence for the L&GBM concept by demonstrating the link between the theoretical model and live application of the ideas. The rollout of the concept initially was quite straightforward—to similar (sister) manufacturing cells. From there, the concept followed classic Lean thinking by deployment across a value stream. The reverse testing provided an opportunity to test the concept in other manufacturing environments where it would seem that all the preconditions for success were in place.

In any large organization, there will be a number of stakeholders and influential people who need to be considered before embarking on any change program.

See Figure 2.1 for the evaluation of the political landscape behind the L&GBM deployment.

Purpose of the L&GBM

Although, according to Bicheno (2000), the purpose of Lean thinking can be described in four main dimensions:

1. safety,
2. quality,
3. delivery, and
4. cost.

Lozano (2008), in his article "Envisioning Sustainability Three-Dimensionally," reviews the concept of environmental sustainability established by several authors and states that the Green thinking can be quoted as

> Use of natural resources without going beyond the carrying capacities and the production of pollutants without passing the biodegradation limits of the receiving system.

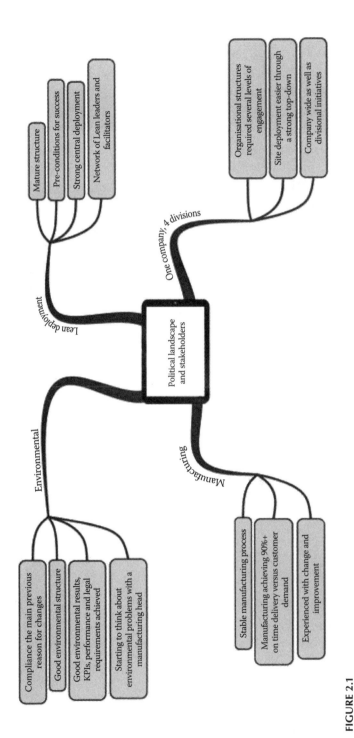

FIGURE 2.1
L&GBM political landscape. (Developed by the authors.)

Therefore, the general purpose of environmental thinking can be described in one dimension (environment), with two main focuses:

1. Using natural resources to maximize productivity
2. Minimum environmental impact

The concept of the L&GBM is linking Lean thinking with environmental problems, adding one more dimension to traditional Lean thinking, the environment. In this context, the main objectives of the model are based on the fundamental building blocks of environmentally sustainable practices:

1. Improving the productivity of manufacturing processes resources by optimizing the environmental performance (materials and energy consumption and wastes generation)
2. Reducing the impact of manufacturing processes on the environment, by reducing all environmental wastes generated by production

Following this, the general purpose of the model can be described as:

Producing exactly what the customer wants, exactly when (with no delay), at a fair price and with minimum waste and environmental impact by delivering the maximum productivity in the use of natural resources.

This means that the Lean and Green thinking can be described in five dimensions:

1. Safety
2. Quality
3. Delivery
4. Cost
5. Environment

as described in Figure 2.2.

Several previous studies comparing Lean and Green practices concluded that environmental practices are the main driver for reaching better environmental performance. Following this, it makes absolute sense that in order to be aligned to sustainability principles; L&GBM suggests Lean thinking is adapted to manage the fundamental building blocks of environmentally sustainable practices:

1. Improving the productivity of manufacturing processes resources
2. Reducing the impact of manufacturing processes environmental

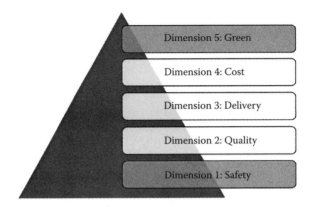

FIGURE 2.2
The five dimensions of the L&GBM. (From Pampanelli, A., L&GBM, PhD Thesis, School of Engineering, UFRGS, Porto Alegre, Brazil, 2013.)

The L&GBM integrates the core characteristics of Green and Lean thinking; therefore, the new model supports the three sustainability dimensions of

1. Profit
2. People
3. Planet

Principles of the L&GBM

In general terms, Green thinking models, such as industrial ecology (Tibbs, 1992; Nielsen, 2007), industrial symbiosis (Boons et al., 2011), ecoefficiency (Korhone, 2007), triple bottom line (Lenzen, 2008), natural capitalism (Hawken et al., 1999; Robèrt, 2002a), and the natural step (Robèrt, 2002b), can be generalized by four common key principles:

1. Identify environmental aspects and impacts.
2. Measure environmental impact and the use of natural resources.
3. Identify alternatives to impact reduction and resources productivity.
4. Continuous Improvement.

Womack and Jones (1996) offer five key principles for defining and describing Lean thinking. In order to operationalize the Lean thinking principles, the identification of value streams is the key first step, to make value flow at the pull of the customer. In Lean enterprises, manufacturing processes are organized in levels of flow, where the three levels are as follows:

1. The first level is the cell level, the lowest production level in a man-ufacturing company organized by Lean principles, composed by a finite number of operations/machines, balanced to achieve one piece flow and maximum people and machine utilization that forms a portion of the total value stream oriented to produce one specific part of the final product requested by customer.

2. The second level is the factory level, value stream level, composed by several cells that are part of the same value stream; because value streams are oriented by customer product families, one factory may possess more than one value stream; value streams exist within the plant aligned to product/process families.

3. The third level is the extended value stream level, composed by several sites (external supplier through to customer) that are part of the same value stream.

Figure 2.3 creates a visual framework of the three levels of flow based on Lean thinking concepts.

The leadership, methodology, and execution patterns, designed for improving value stream performance in an organization that applies Lean thinking as a strategy for increasing manufacturing performance, are used in the L&GBM. The difference here is that, instead of focusing on improving the flow of value (i.e., the main goal of improving manufacturing performance), the focus is on optimizing the use of the value stream supporting flows of mass and energy. Following this, the L&GBM can be described by five key principles:

1. *Identify a stable value stream (VS):* Identify a stable value stream (level 1, 2, or 3). A stable value stream is a value stream that copes with the main dimensions of Lean thinking: (1) safety, (2) quality, (3) delivery, and (4) cost.

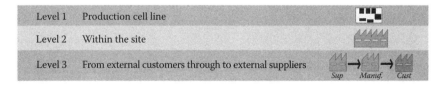

Level 1	Production cell line
Level 2	Within the site
Level 3	From external customers through to external suppliers

FIGURE 2.3
Manufacturing three level of flow based for Lean thinking organizations. (From Pampanelli, A., L&GBM, PhD Thesis, School of Engineering, UFRGS, Porto Alegre, Brazil, 2013.)

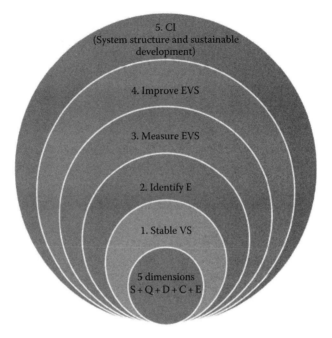

FIGURE 2.4

The principles of the L&GBM. (From Pampanelli, A., L&GBM, PhD Thesis, School of Engineering, UFRGS, Porto Alegre, Brazil, 2013.)

2. *Identify the environmental impact (E):* Identify in the chosen value stream the environmental aspects and impacts.
3. *Measure the environmental value streams (EVS):* Measure the value stream environmental impacts and the use of natural resources (the value stream mass and energy flows).
4. *Improve the environmental value streams (EVS):* Identify alternatives to (1) impact reduction and (2) resources productivity within the value stream.
5. *Continuous Improvement (CI):* Set alternatives for improving the value stream supporting mass and energy flows.

Figure 2.4 illustrates the integration of these ideas and presents the overall concept of the L&GBM principles.

Ways of Working of the L&GBM

As the idea of the L&GBM is using a Lean thinking philosophy to solve environmental problems, the main objectives of the model are based on the fundamental building blocks of Green thinking practices. Following this, the two main objectives of L&GBM are

1. Improving manufacturing processes resources productivity by optimizing its supporting flows performance (materials and energy consumption and wastes generation)
2. Reducing manufacturing processes environmental impact, by reducing all environmental wastes generated by production

Therefore, the substance of study of the L&GBM is the mass–energy flows of the manufacturing processes. The expected output for the application of the model is the achievement of improvements in these thermodynamic flows (materials, chemicals, water, waste, effluent, and energy), contributing to the improvement of the overall performance of the system. There are many potential cost savings associated with reducing the environmental impact of a business, for example, reducing the consumption of harmful chemicals and energy will impact directly on overheads, as well as reducing safety and environmental risks to the employees and the surrounding area.

In this sense, the basic and most important idea of the L&GBM is integrating the Green approaches as part of the continuous improvement process of a manufacturing process, where the Lean philosophy and ways of working are already in place. The subjects of study of the L&GBM are the mass–energy flows of the manufacturing processes.

The fundamental building block of Lean thinking is continuous improvement. Kaizen, with its focus on problem solving and employee involvement fits perfectly with the notion of creating a Greener industry. The L&GBM takes a Kaizen approach to understanding and improving the environmental flows of mass and energy of manufacturing a cell and the value stream. The key difference being that instead of focusing on the flow of product (which is the main goal of improving manufacturing performance), the focus of L&GBM is on optimizing the use of the mass and energy flows across the value stream. For L&GBM, data collection and the data collection structure is a key prerequisite for the Kaizen event. Apart from the physical presence of waste materials, none of the other environmental flows can be visualized and hence calculated, so prework preparation and data collection are important key steps and should be comprehensively developed in order to achieve good results from the Kaizen event.

L&GBM Is Different from Pure Lean and Green Thinking

Following the description of the L&GBM developed in sections "The Purpose of the L&GBM," "The Principles of the L&GBM," and "The Ways of Working of the L&GBM," Table 2.1 highlights the fundamental differences of the L&GBM compared with pure Green and pure Lean thinking in terms of purpose, principles, and ways of working of the dealing of the sustainability vectors (people, profit, and planet).

As can be seen in the table, L&GBM is different from pure Green thinking due to the following:

- *L&GBM prioritizes the customer focus:* In order to deliver L&GBM, it is necessary to be Lean first; therefore, a prerequisite of the L&GBM is the implementation of Lean to deployment level.
- *L&GBM identifies and measures environmental aspects and impacts based on value stream thinking:* Traditional Green thinking does not focus on the manufacturing ways of working.
- *L&GBM focuses on a top-down and bottom-up approach:* For deploying environmental continuous improvements.
- *L&GBM prioritizes maximizing value and reducing costs:* It has an environmental approach, prioritizing financial savings and waste reduction as well.

When we compare L&GBM with pure Lean thinking, L&GBM is different from pure Lean thinking due to the following:

- *L&GBM introduces into the traditional Lean thinking a new dimension—the environmental concern aspect:* Traditional Lean thinking focuses on four dimensions, namely, safety, quality, delivery, and cost. L&GBM introduces the environmental concern, requiring
  1. Minimization of the use of resources
  2. Reduction of environmental impact
  3. The need of environmental awareness along the flow of value
- *L&GBM focus in other sources of savings:* Traditional Lean thinking considers only reduction of the seven classic wastes. With the introduction of the environmental variable concern along the flow of value, other sources of wastes may be evaluated and reduced, maximizing the overall savings.

TABLE 2.1

Table Comparing L&GBM with Pure Lean and Pure Green Thinking

	Green: Environmental Sustainability Thinking	Lean: Lean Thinking	L&GBM
General purpose	"Use of natural resources without going beyond the carrying capacities and the production of pollutants without passing the biodegradation limits of the receiving system" (Lozano, 2008)	"Producing exactly what the customer wants, exactly when (with no delay), at fair price and minimum waste" (Bicheno, 2000)	"Producing exactly what the customer wants, exactly when (with no delay), at fair price and minimum waste and environmental impact and the maximum productivity in the use of natural resources"
Main principles	1. Identify environmental aspects and impacts 2. Measure environmental impact and the use of natural resources 3. Identify alternatives to (1) impact reduction and (2) resources productivity 4. Continuous improvement	1. Specific value 2. Identify value streams 3. Make value flow 4. Let the customer pull value 5. Pursue perfection (Womack and Jones, 1998)	1. Identify a stable value stream (level 1, 2, or 3) 2. Identify in the flow of value the environmental aspects and impacts 3. Measure VS environmental impacts and the use of natural resources 4. Identify alternatives to (1) impact reduction and (2) resources productivity in VS 5. Pursue perfection—continuous improvement
People	1. Environmental awareness in all levels of the organization 2. High level of technical competence for people responsible for environmental impacts	1. Leadership (top-down) 2. Kaizen (bottom-up) People involvement and creation of solving problems culture	1. Leadership (top-down) 2. Kaizen (bottom-up) 3. Environmental awareness along the flow of value

(Continued)

TABLE 2.1 (*Continued*)

Table Comparing L&GBM with Pure Lean and Pure Green Thinking

	Green: Environmental Sustainability Thinking	Lean: Lean Thinking	L&GBM
Profit	1. Equity (economic/ environmental)	1. Maximize financial savings (revenue) 2. Reduce waste	1. Maximize financial savings (revenue) 2. Reduce waste (for all sources of wastes streams) 3. Equity (economic/ environmental)
Planet	1. Productivity in the use of natural resources (mass and energy) 2. Environmental impact reduction (3Rs)	None	1. Productivity in the use of natural resources (mass and energy) 2. Environmental impact reduction (3Rs)

Source: Pampanelli, A., L&GBM, PhD Thesis, School of Engineering, UFRGS, Porto Alegre, Brazil, 2013.

In fact, the overall idea of the L&GBM encompasses the same principles of the Lean thinking that are set in the house of Lean, where the stability is the base. Kaizen is one of the main pillars with the ultimate goal of improving performance that, in this case, is based on four dimensions:

1. S—Safety
2. Q—Quality
3. D—Delivery
4. C—Cost

The difference is that one more dimension, (E) environment, is added to existing model as shown in Figure 2.5.

In fact, Rich (2006) discusses Lean improvement stages from chaos to control competitive advantage, setting the natural steps to be followed by a manufacturing process implementing Lean principles over a period of time. By concentrating first on stabilizing processes, where the basic disciplines of safety and morale is addressed, followed by improvements in quality, delivery performance, and process flexibility,

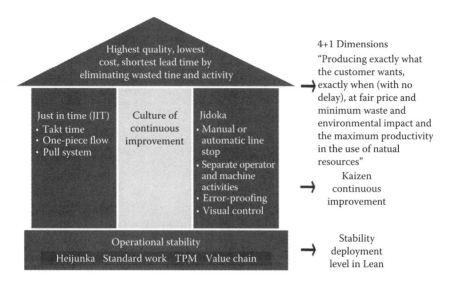

FIGURE 2.5

The house of Lean and the L&GBM. (Adapted from Rich, N., Understanding the Lean journey, in N. Rich, N. Bateman, A. Esain, L. Massey, and D. Samuel, eds., *Evolution of Lean: Lessons from the Workplace*, Cambridge University Press, Cambridge, U.K., 2006, pp. 11–31.)

costs are reduced naturally, creating opportunities for further cost reduction that are realized in the later stages:

Process stability (safety + quality + delivery + flexibility) → cost reduction

Perhaps, this logic does not take into consideration the other sources of cost that are part of the manufacturing process, the environmental wastes (materials and energy consumption and wastes generation) that are not considered in the original Rich's model. Therefore, the L&GBM is built based on Rich's model, adding one extra variable to it:

Process stability (safety + quality + delivery + flexibility) + environment → cost reduction

Consolidating the L&GBM

Table 2.2 highlights the general characteristics of the L&GBM for the three levels of product flows.

One of the first tasks in developing any change program in a large multi-international corporation is achieving wider engagement and

TABLE 2.2

Main Characteristics of the L&GBM for the Three Levels of Flows

	Level 1 Flow	Level 2 Flow	Level 3 Flow
	Improving manufacturing processes resources productivity by optimizing its supporting flows performance (materials and energy consumption and wastes generation) Reducing manufacturing processes environmental impact by reducing environmental wastes generated by production		
Main objectives of system output	*Improve supporting flows performance in cell level:* materials, chemicals, water, waste, effluent, and energy	*Improve supporting flows performance in factory level:* materials, chemicals, water, waste, effluent, energy, CO_2, package, etc. Establishment of local/factory new environmental strategies	Improvement of extended product flow performance: raw materials, chemicals, toxic elements, water, waste, effluent, energy, CO_2, package, etc. Establishment of global environmental strategies.
Object of study	*Cell-supporting flows:* materials, chemicals, water, waste, effluent, energy	*Factory-supporting flows:* materials, chemicals, water, waste, effluent, energy, CO_2, package, etc.	*Extended product-supporting flows:* raw materials, chemicals, toxic elements, water, waste, effluent, energy, CO_2, package, etc.
General main prerequisites for the L&GBM	1. Cell that has a mature deployment level in using and applying Lean tools	1. Factory has an overall mature deployment level in using and applying Lean tools	1. Factories involved in the eVSM have an overall mature deployment level in using and applying Lean tools
	2. Cell has a stable process, with delivery records over 90%	2. Factory has a stable process, with delivery records over 90%	2. eVSM process is stable, with an average delivery records over 90%
	3. Cell that has already applied EI systems	3. EI	3. EI
	4. A management team is supporting the Lean and Green initiative	4. A management team (plant manager) is supporting the Lean and Green initiative	4. A management team (VSM managers/ directors) is supporting the Lean and Green initiative

(Continued)

TABLE 2.2 (*Continued*)

Main Characteristics of the L&GBM for the Three Levels of Flows

	Level 1 Flow	Level 2 Flow	Level 3 Flow
	5. Good level of environmental awareness/concern exists	5. Factory is ISO 14001 certified and it is in its second improvement cycle	5. Factories that are part of the extended flow are ISO 14001 certified: second improvement cycle
	6. Cell has a significant use of resources	6. Factory has a significant use of resources (materials, chemicals, water, waste, effluent, and energy)	6. Factories have a significant use of resources
	7. Structure in place for environmental data collection	7. Structure in place for environmental data collection	7. Structure in place for environmental data collection

Source: Pampanelli, A., L&GBM, PhD Thesis, School of Engineering, UFRGS, Porto Alegre, Brazil, 2013.

buy-in to the concept. In the case of L&GBM, it is no different. The first engagement group identified was what we can call the "technical supporters." These are the people who represent the local "technical" connection to the concept in question and in this case were the *environmental managers*. The other option would have been to connect with the Lean network, the regional/site continuous-improvement leaders. The global environmental managers were chosen in preference to the local and regional continuous-improvement leaders for the initial engagement session. Their technical and legislative knowledge is a key specialist skill that was required to be part of the L&GBM activities. Without these individuals, the workshops would not succeed. In terms of the regional and site continuous improvement leaders, as consequence of their training, they tended to be more supportive of change processes and were very keen to try out new concepts. The support of the regional and local CI leaders was not taken for granted, but evaluated as being part way along the change curve, as a result this group were engaged later in the process.

The objective of the engagement session with the global environmental managers was

- To communicate the basic concepts of the program
- To share the process of improvement
- To gain their input to the workshop structure
- To identify potential benefits and barriers of implementation
- To gain their support
- To use this network for wider global communication

After the initial communication of the project, the environmental managers were asked to brainstorm and then to prioritize the benefits and potential barriers to implementation. The group then identified the 10 key success factors and 10 key challenges to implementation. This information provided useful to address the barriers and challenges to implementation going forward.

Table 2.3 presents the benefits and barriers for rolling out the L&GBM across the group as defined by the global environmental managers' team.

It can be seen from the table that there were almost as many barriers to implementation as there were benefits. This feedback identified the challenges of deployment for the project; it was interesting to note that these challenges came from the group of people most closely associated with championing environmental thinking within the organization, where it might be expected that the group would generate more benefits than barriers considering their background and area of expertise. Figure 2.6 highlights 10 success factors and 10 challenges for implementation identified by the global environmental managers' team.

While the engagement session helped to identify the benefits and barriers to the L&GBM initiative, it also helped to psychologically move the environmental managers from ambivalent fence sitters to being supporters of the project—now they had the opportunity to air their fears and to input into the project. The success factors were used as part of the later discussion to "sell" the concept to key stakeholders around the business. This was achieved not through articulating an elevator speech in a chance meeting with senior leaders, but more by guiding conversations to understand what real issues exist for the plant directors and relating how the L&GBM initiative could help them achieve their business objectives. The barriers were used to develop a set of countermeasures and implementation guidelines to ensure success in the pilot implementation.

TABLE 2.3

Benefits and Barriers for Rolling Out the L&GBM

Sustainability Vectors	Benefits	Barriers
Planet	1. *Environmental concern is key for today's business:* "Environment, especially in Europe, is an important point: Customers and stakeholders will push us to improve. Avoiding and reducing waste is one of our main topics in our yearly environmental program."	1. *Access to technology:* "Many new technologies available, but payback is prohibitive (more than 3 years). Design of products does not normally consider the energy required to make the product. Access to new technologies not universally available— developing countries; Solar, bio-fuels, wind turbines, recycling of heat, building insulation—all come at cost without clear profitability."
	2. *Creating a new paradigm— Lean to Green concept:* "It was proved that a manufacturing team with a good Lean system in place has a solid platform for developing environmental improvements in a sustainable way."	2. *Lack of integration of environment into Lean:* "The way our Lean training is developed now doesn't appear to encompass environmental savings."
	3. *Recreating the concept of cleaner production:* "A fresh approach to resurrecting an old topic— most of us have been preaching and/working on Green since the mid-1990s. This reinvigorates the process and the thinking."	3. *Environment differences worldwide:* "Wide gaps between global, region, country and districts— people will generally comply with the local legislation, but not go further. Access to best in class technologies is not available (even basics like water and power in India, for example). More pressure from local authorities becoming evident— is this good for the company or just costly? Global energy costs rising, but alternatives are governed by what is locally available (Gas, Oil, LPG, etc.)."

(Continued)

TABLE 2.3 (*Continued*)

Benefits and Barriers for Rolling Out the L&GBM

Sustainability Vectors	Benefits	Barriers
	4. *Improve the use of resources:* "By improving the flow of resources within the manufacturing cell—great potential for reducing environmental impact."	None
	5. *An alternative for pollution prevention:* "Use environmentally sustainable practices for addressing pollution prevention initiatives integrated to Lean."	None
People	1. *An integrated and systematic approach:* "Project combined (1) Employee Engagement, (2) Lean Kaizen approach, (3) Problem Solving and Project Management; (4) Green environmental thinking."	1. *Lack of awareness by management of real costs and savings potential.*
	2. *A team effort:* "More thoughts, more potential, more successes; Greater number of people involved in environmental activities—greater understanding and more hands to do the work. Use of Employee engagement tools and soft skills for capturing the best ideas."	2. *Lack of expertise throughout the organization to direct and guide; lack of implementers to do L&GBM.*
	3. *Supporting CI culture:* "Integrates environmental thinking into Lean activities instead of it being seen as stand-alone—someone else's job."	3. *Cultural differences:* "Many different sites having different cultures, different history, different environment."

(Continued)

TABLE 2.3 (*Continued*)

Benefits and Barriers for Rolling Out the L&GBM

Sustainability Vectors	Benefits	Barriers
Profit	1. *Cost reduction approach— optimize the use of resources:* "Lean is recognized and committed to within the organization—adapting this proven route is a recipe for success—Lean techniques have now gained high efficiency and credibility—it will be good approach if we can adapt the tools to Green and prove effectiveness."	1. *Cost priorities:* "Many things to do—no quick wins. Focus on customer and profits. Pressure to reduce headcount. Satisfying stakeholders in the shorter term. Lack of clarity on our priorities and at the same time, too many initiatives we need to support or at least consider."
	2. *Improve overall results:* "Looks at the process from start to finish finding opportunities for environmental savings. Therefore, improve overall results (environmental, costs, use of resources, etc.) in a more focused, business oriented approach."	2. *Manufacturing priorities:* "All Lean activities need to happen against a basic need to retain sufficient time to make production schedules."
	3. *Operational focus:* "Lean has operational focus; we really measure our performance on PCDA (Plan-Do-Check-Act) basis. We can do the same with the L&GBM."	3. *Lack of resources:* "Competition for time, experts and priority. There's a lot going on simultaneously. We must also keep in mind that the downturn pushed us to restrict our resources very significantly. Lean tools development used a large amount of resources and time."

Source: Pampanelli, A., L&GBM, PhD Thesis, School of Engineering, UFRGS, Porto Alegre, Brazil, 2013.

UNDERSTANDING THE L&GBM KAIZENS

The agenda for the Kaizen was developed from previous structures used for both manufacturing and business process Kaizen events. The content was focused on L&GBM with the emphasis on what could be achieved for the environment through this approach. Table 2.4 presents the summary of a Kaizen agenda.

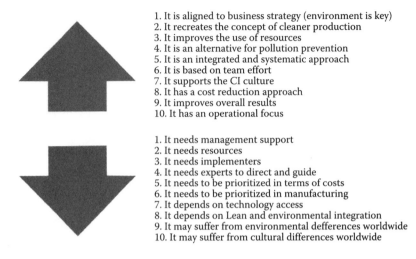

1. It is aligned to business strategy (environment is key)
2. It recreates the concept of cleaner production
3. It improves the use of resources
4. It is an alternative for pollution prevention
5. It is an integrated and systematic approach
6. It is based on team effort
7. It supports the CI culture
8. It has a cost reduction approach
9. It improves overall results
10. It has an operational focus

1. It needs management support
2. It needs resources
3. It needs implementers
4. It needs experts to direct and guide
5. It needs to be prioritized in terms of costs
6. It needs to be prioritized in manufacturing
7. It depends on technology access
8. It depends on Lean and environmental integration
9. It may suffer from environmental defferences worldwide
10. It may suffer from cultural differences worldwide

FIGURE 2.6
Ten success factors and 10 challenges for L&GBM. (From Pampanelli, A., L&GBM, PhD Thesis, School of Engineering, UFRGS, Porto Alegre, Brazil, 2013.)

The agenda for the workshop was constructed using the standard Kaizen template, adapted to the requirements for a L&GBM workshop. The key difference between a standard mapping exercise and the L&GB workshop was the amount of prework required to define and collect the relevant environmental flows. Various meters had to be installed alongside existing manual and automated tracking systems to capture flow and usage rates for power, gas, water, air, and chemicals as well as product scrap and by-products. These data were collected for a month prior to the workshop to provide the group with meaningful data to interrogate during the workshop. For L&GBM analysis the data needs to be available prior to the workshop to do be able to the Kaizen—this contrasts with value stream mapping or other Lean tools where data is collected as part of the workshop. The data requirements are more onerous for L&GBM as they cannot be seen nor readily quantified—one look at a power cable will say nothing about the electricity use whereas a pallet of parts can be counted and attributed with VSM.

The team was further aligned to environmental thinking by assigning people to evaluate a specific environmental flow through the cell. The impact of this process was to generate ownership for each environmental flow to work out its impact and also work on deploying the improvement

TABLE 2.4

L&GBM for a Cell—Kaizen Agenda

Activity #	Topic	Timing	Responsibility	Resources
1	Welcome, concepts, and activities	30 min	Project leader	Presentation and group dynamics activity
2	Environmental waste concept review—current state analyses	30 min	Environmental specialist	Environmental wastes Current state map
3	Project scope review—environmental prioritization		Lean leaders	Scoping document Prioritization matrix and structure
4	Team work—definition of teams by environmental flow, participants, and leaders	30 min	Lean leaders	Data sheets with environmental flow data analysis sheets
5	Shop floor review—cell waste analysis by team	1 h 30 min	Team leaders	Data sheets with VSM's data waste analysis sheets action plan sheets
	Break			
6	Team waste analysis consolidation	30 min	Team leaders	Consolidation sheet, brown paper, post-it notes, pens
7	Team future state map development	30 min	Team leaders	Consolidation sheet, brown paper, post-it notes, pens
8	Team waste action plan development	30 min	Team leaders	Action plan worksheet
9	Team action plan and future state environmental flow presentation and validation with management team	1 h	Team leaders	Environmental flows and action plan worksheets
10	Workshop results/data analysis	15 min	CI leader	Cost analysis worksheet Consolidate action plan worksheet

(Continued)

TABLE 2.4 (Continued)

L&GBM for a Cell—Kaizen Agenda

Activity #	Topic	Timing	Responsibility	Resources
11	Closing remarks— workshop results analysis (employee involvement perspective)	15 min	Managers and project leaders	Free debate
		6 h		

Source: Pampanelli, A., L&GBM, PhD Thesis, School of Engineering, UFRGS, Porto Alegre, Brazil, 2013.

actions from the workshop. We had created the culture for people to "fight" for their respective environmental corners.

1. *Welcome, concepts, and activities:* This involved a welcome and introduction to the Kaizen workshop. The introduction to the workshop was achieved through the creation of a mind map to answer the following questions:
   - Their expectations about the Kaizen results
   - The perceived benefits of implementing L&GBM
   - The main barriers for deploying this concept

   An example of a completed mind map from one of the Kaizen events is presented in Figure 2.7.

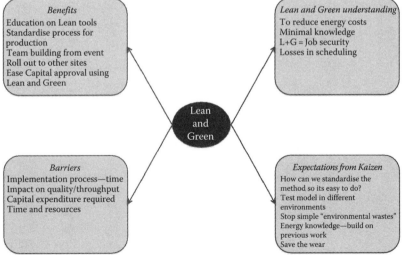

FIGURE 2.7
Example of a Kaizen mind map. (Developed by the authors.)

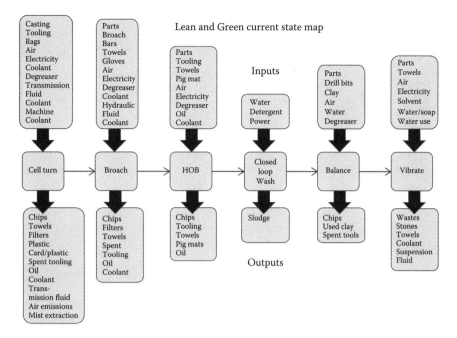

FIGURE 2.8
Example of L&GBM current state map. (Developed by the authors.)

These mind maps help to frame the workshop and enable the facilitators to adjust the content of the workshop at an early stage depending on the answers to the questions posed at the start of the brainstorm.

2. *Environmental wastes concept review—Current state analysis:* In this session the environmental specialists created a L&GBM value stream map, as shown in Figure 2.8.

Figure 2.9 presents a real example.

This map process provided a visual representation of the environmental inputs and outputs for the chosen process. This format was used to engage the team with the objective of getting the team to identify the environmental flows and understand the opportunity to reduce the wastes.

3. *Project scope review:* In this session the overall scope of the project is defined. The previously created overall process map is reviewed and the boundaries of the specific workshop are defined. This typically

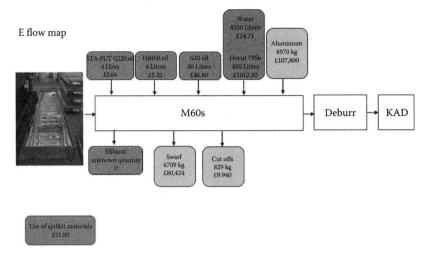

FIGURE 2.9
Example of a simple e-flow Map. (Developed by the authors.)

would restrict the workshop to a number of machines in an area or a value stream in a factory. The scope defines the following:

- The people who need to be involved
- The different departments that need to be involved
- The stakeholders, customers, and suppliers to the process
- The start and end points of the process under L&GBM review
- The measures and targets
- The objectives

The scope needs to be agreed by the group to ensure full buy-in to the workshop and also be underwritten by the site management team as the key group of stakeholders for the Kaizen activity.

4. *Definition of teams:* The team is now split up into smaller groups. The team has a cross representation of the various different departments involved in manufacturing. This cross functional grouping allowed a broad skills base to analyze each waste flow. Each group is allocated a specific environmental flow to analyze. They are provided with environmental flow data to check and review.

5. *Shop floor review:* In this session the groups walk the manufacturing process on the shop floor. They capture the data for their particular environmental flow on the waste analysis sheets and also create ideas for improvement—how to reduce the environmental wastes/use in

FIGURE 2.10
Example of waste that teams need to identify at the shop floor. (Developed by the authors.)

their flow. Figure 2.10 presents an example of the type of waste team need to identify at the shop floor.

6. *Team waste analysis:* All the wastes are now consolidated onto one sheet. Figure 2.11 presents the main analysis teams need to develop.

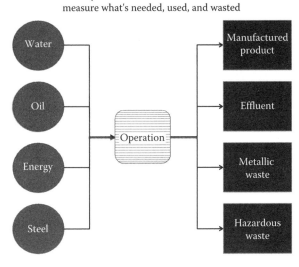

FIGURE 2.11
Teams' shop floor analysis. (Developed by the authors.)

7. *Team future state:* Using the consolidation sheet, a future state is developed. This makes a step change in environmental performance for the area under review.

8. *Team waste action plan:* The team reviews the actions required to deliver the future state and remove the environmental wastes. It creates an action plan—what, who, when, and status to help drive the implementation.

9. *Report back to Leadership:* The final outcomes of the workshop are presented to the leadership team for review, validation, and support. This gives the project wider visibility and an opportunity to integrate with the wider activities within the factory.

10. *Workshop results:* The workshop results (i.e., identified potential benefits) are summarized alongside the action plan—providing leadership a key indication of what they get for their investment in the action plan. Once the 6-h Kaizen event was complete, the teams that were participating defined new future state, identifying improvement opportunities for each cell. Typical improvements that were identified included
    - Reduction in packaging through redesign
    - Reduction in power use through better working methods
    - Elimination of steps no longer required
    - Review of product design to reduce off cuts
    - Installation of timers and energy-saving devices—lights/motion detectors.

11. *Closing summary:* The senior management sponsor closes the session recognizing the time and effort of the team members.

L&GBM FOR A CELL

The cell is the lowest production level in a manufacturing company organized around Lean principles, and it is composed of a finite number of operations or machines. The key objective of developing the L&GBM at the cell level is to improve the performance of the supporting environmental flows (i.e., materials and energy consumption and waste generation) and to reduce all waste and impacts. The heart of this study is the mass–energy flows of the cell, which are evaluated according to operation. The expected output is improvement in these flows. Figure 2.12 describes the study's framework.

The basic, and most important, idea behind the L&GBM is that Lean and Green approaches can be integrated as part of a continuous improvement

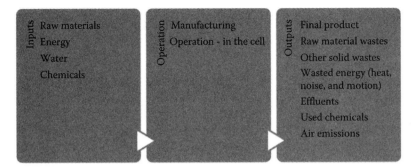

FIGURE 2.12
Mass and energy flow analysis using the L&GBM at the cell level. (From Pampanelli, A., L&GBM, PhD Thesis, School of Engineering, UFRGS, Porto Alegre, Brazil, 2013.)

process at a cell where Lean manufacturing is already in place. Therefore, the main prerequisites for a cell to be a candidate for the L&GBM are as follows:

1. A stable process, with delivery records over 90% (this figure is relative to the industry; for other sectors stability may be deemed a higher or lower level)
2. A mature deployment level in using and applying Lean tools (i.e., operators already know and apply the most common Lean tools such as 5S, visual management, autonomous maintenance, and lost time analysis)
3. Employee involvement (EI) systems are in place (operators already know and apply the most team involving common EI tools, such as daily meeting, primary visual display, weekly meetings, recognition, etc.)
4. A supportive management team (i.e., a cell manager as well as middle and senior management) is available to sponsor the Lean and Green initiative
5. Good level of environmental awareness (i.e., operators have already been trained in understanding related environment issues and concerns)
6. Significant use of natural resources (i.e., materials, chemicals, water, and energy)
7. Structure in place for environmental data collection

Based on Lean thinking, the L&GBM involves five steps, presented in Figure 2.13.

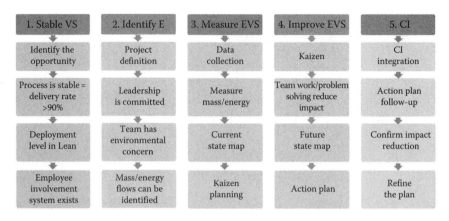

FIGURE 2.13
The five-step L&GBM for improving the performance of supporting flows in a production cell. (From Pampanelli, A., L&GBM, PhD Thesis, School of Engineering, UFRGS, Porto Alegre, Brazil, 2013.)

The objective of each step is described now:

Step 1—Stable value stream (VS): Identify the need for improvement. Identify an operational cell that represents a significant use of resources, has a good deployment of Lean tools, and has a stable production flow that justifies application of the L&GBM.

Step 2—Identify environmental characteristics and impacts (E): Define the process improvement scope by identifying the environmental aspects and impacts of the value stream (in this case, the cell). Characteristic and impact definitions are considered according to ISO 14001:2004 (International Organization for Standardization (ISO), 2004). An environmental characteristic is a feature or aspect of an activity, product, or service that affects or can affect the environment, the cell inputs, or the cell outputs. An environmental impact is a change to the environment caused by environmental characteristics resulting from cell inputs and outputs.

Step 3—Measure environmental value streams (EVS): Identify the actual data on the environmental process. Collect environmental data. Map the cell "as-is" (i.e., the current state of the process) and identify the cell's actual state for its main environmental flows. Measure the mass–energy flows for the cell. Organize the Kaizen event. The improvement metrics used for this Kaizen event are as follows:

- Energy: Use of meters for collecting all energy consumed in a specific period of time (i.e., month). Energy invoices are used to determine the cost.

- Water: Use of meters for collecting all water consumed in a specific period of time (i.e., month). Water invoices are used to determine the cost.
- Metallic and contaminated waste and other waste: This represents all types of waste produced by a cell in a specific period of time (i.e., month). Waste invoices are used to determine the cost.
- Oils and chemicals: A company material system (i.e., oracle, ERP system) is used to access all chemicals used by a cell in a specific period of time (i.e., month). Invoices are used to determine the cost.
- Effluents: Use of meters for collecting all effluent generated in a specific period of time (i.e., month). Invoices are used to determine the cost.

Step 4—Improve environmental value streams (EVS): Identify waste elimination opportunities during a Kaizen workshop. Prioritize the main production supporting flows for the team to analyze during the Kaizen event. Organize teamwork on the shop floor to identify the main waste elimination opportunities, analyze the main waste in each flow, and identify the main improvements. Depending on the size of the cell, in terms of operations and machines, the Kaizen event may involve between 20 and 30 people, including all cell operators, leaders, and managers, and maintenance people as well as environmental and Lean specialists. Figure 2.14 demonstrates the different groups of people that are involved in the Kaizen initiative.

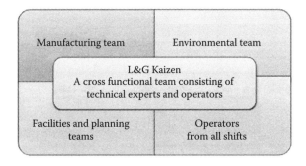

FIGURE 2.14
Groups of people that are involved in the Kaizen initiative—for a cell. (From Pampanelli, A., L&GBM, PhD Thesis, School of Engineering, UFRGS, Porto Alegre, Brazil, 2013.)

The basic Kaizen structure under the L&GBM for a cell includes the following phases:

- *Phase 1:* Devote sufficient time—approximately 2 h to introducing the cell and its actual state and the costs and the environmental impacts of the cell mass and energy flows and then organizing the cross-functional teams that will be responsible for each of the cell's supporting flows (i.e., energy, waste, water, chemicals, etc.).
- *Phase 2:* Devote sufficient time—approximately 2 h to the team-work shop floor exercise. The objective of each team is to understand the use or generation flow of the team's resource during each cell operation. The questions that the teams should answer include the following:
  a. Why is this manufacturing operation necessary in this process?
  b. Why is this waste/consumption generated here?
  c. What is the frequency at which it is generated?
  d. Why is this frequency necessary?
  e. Is this operation deployed in accordance with the work standard?
  f. Is the standard correct?
  g. What can be done to eliminate or reduce this usage?
- *Phase 3:* Devote sufficient time—approximately 2 h to consolidating a future state map for the cell's mass and energy flows and to developing an action plan for improvement opportunities. Some of the questions that should be answered here include the following:
  a. What was identified?
  b. What are the improvement opportunities?
  c. What are the expected changes?
  d. What are the gains?
  e. What does the future state look like?

After answering these questions and after building the new mass/energy map for the cell with a specific action plan for accomplishing these changes, the Kaizen results are presented to the site leadership to approve the plan. Finally, a "to-be" map is developed that shows the future process by considering all the information developed during the Kaizen event.

Step 5—Continuous improvement (CI): Develop prioritized action and communication plans in the Kaizen workshop. The sustainability of the results achieved in the Kaizen should be evaluated through leadership standard work (LSW—Leader's standard work or leadership validation).

The action plan is validated with the project team leader and the Kaizen event action plan is consolidated. Connections between team members are established by applying the EI tools that are already in place. The key learning points from the event, both "areas for improvement" and "what went well," are captured.

Integrating Lean and Green manufacturing is treated a second step in a cell's continuous improvement process. It is understood that a stable production flow is the first step toward achieving a Lean and Green enterprise. Once cell stability is reached and production efficiency is under control, then the team is ready for the next step; this explains why the L&GBM is designated for cells that already have stable production flow and have achieved a benchmark deployment level in applying Lean thinking concepts. In addition, leadership is a fundamental building block for Lean and Green deployment. The Kaizen initiative needs to be approved by cell manager, and it requires the complete commitment of team leaders and team members to deploy it properly. Senior leaders also need to play a role in demonstrating visible sponsorship of the project and performing a check-act on the implementation of the action plan as part of their leadership standard work.

Pilot Testing: L&GBM for a Cell

The pilot testing presented in this section was developed in the GKN Driveline operations in Brazil. The original model tested during the pilot testing was the same presented in this section. The L&GBM pilot testing was developed to investigate the benefits this could have on the environment and the business, in terms of waste reduction, operational performance, and employee commitment. The main objectives of the pilot testing of the L&GBM in a cell were

1. To confirm the five steps proposed as well as the overall structure before rolling it out for several other manufacturing cells
2. To confirm the Lean prerequisites and participants
3. Analyzing potential savings in terms of environmental improvements and cost reduction after applying the model
4. Identifying model improvement opportunities

Following this, GKN Driveline in Brazil developed a pilot application for the L&GBM for a cell. The pilot project was developed in model cells (Cell 1 and Cell 2) with deployment level of Lean via a cross-functional

Kaizen team event to ensure that all the team members were fully involved and had the opportunity to contribute their ideas.

Table 2.5 presents basic characteristics of the manufacturing operational cells where the L&GBM was applied.

The pilot Kaizen events were developed at the end of 2008 and 2010, following the five-step model presented in Figure 2.13. After identifying the need for improvement and having the Kaizen model testing approved and backed by the organization's leadership, a period of data collection took place with support from facilities and environmental specialists. The data was collected in accordance with the following structure:

- *Energy:* Use of meters for collecting all energy consumed in a specific period of time (i.e., month). Energy invoices were used to determine the cost.
- *Water:* Use of meters for collecting all water consumed in a specific period of time (i.e., month). Water invoices were used to determine the cost.
- *Metallic and contaminated waste and other waste:* This represents all types of waste produced by a cell in a specific period of time (i.e., month). They were all weighed to determine the quantity. Waste invoices were used to determine the cost.
- *Oils and chemicals:* A company materials requirements planning system is used to access all chemicals used by a cell in a specific period of time (i.e. a month). Invoices were used to determine the cost.
- *Effluents:* Use of meters for collecting all effluent generated in a specific period of time (i.e., month). Invoices were used to determine the cost.

The Kaizen structure was organized with the data in order to analyze and review the actual state for the mass and energy flows of the studied cells. The Kaizen events involved around 30 people, including all cell operators, leaders and managers, maintenance people, as well as EHS and Lean specialists. The basic Kaizen event agenda presented in Table 2.4 was followed.

After a 6-h Kaizen event with the objective of reducing cost, waste, and consumption of natural resources for different production mass and energy flows (energy, metallic waste, chemical products, hazards waste, effluents, and water), the teams that were participating in either of the pilot events defined a new future, identifying improvement opportunities for each of the cell's supporting flows. The results delivered from the Kaizens are shown in Table 2.6.

TABLE 2.5

Environmental and Manufacturing Characteristics of the Pilot Cells Where the L&GBM Was Applied

Manufacturing Characteristics	Cell 1	Cell 2
Location	Brazil factory 1	Brazil factory 1
Nature of operations	Steel machining of parts for producing a monobloc (part of a half-shaft)	Assembly of manufactured parts for producing a half-shaft
Main cell mass and energy flows	Energy	Energy
	Water	Waste grease
	Chemicals/oils	Hazardous wastes
	Effluents	Cleaning cloths
	Metallic waste	
	Hazardous wastes	
Actual state data: energy and materials consumption and wastes generation	Energy consumption: 261 MWh/month	Energy consumption: 11 MWh/month
	Water consumption: 1.4 m³/month	Waste grease: 0.2 ton/month
	Chemicals usage: 0.6 m³/month	Hazardous wastes: 3 m³/month
	Metallic wastes: 55 ton/month	Cleaning cloths usage: 3120 units/month
	Hazardous wastes: 60 m³/month	
Analysis of prerequisites		
Level of Lean	Deployment level	Deployment level
Process stability	90%	90%
Application of employee involvement tools	In place	In place
Leadership support	High	High
Environmental awareness	In place	In place
Use of resources	High	Medium
Structure for data collection	In place	In place
Total cost of mass and energy flows (US$/year)	$1,005,000	$483,500
Major impact in the cell environmental cost	Metallic waste 68%	Grease 75%

Source: Pampanelli, A., L&GBM, PhD Thesis, School of Engineering, UFRGS, Porto Alegre, Brazil, 2013.

TABLE 2.6

Results of the Two Pilot Kaizen events: Percentage of Reductions

Cell Impact	Cell 1	Cell 2
Energy	8%	6%
General chemical products consumption	91% (oils)	1% (grease in the product)
Water consumption	34%	NA
Effluent generation	69%	NA
Metallic waste generation	33%	NA
Hazardous waste generation	67%	45%
Cleaning cloths	NA	50%
Grease waste generation	NA	100%[a]
Average resources	50%	40%

Source: Pampanelli, A., L&GBM, PhD Thesis, School of Engineering, UFRGS, Porto Alegre, Brazil, 2013.

NA, not applicable.

[a] 100% waste elimination due to 100% recycling of grease.

One of the key enablers to successful implementation was the system for tracking the deployment of the action plan. This involved a regular check by the leadership on the deployment of the actions. The leaders invested time in checking and, most importantly, coaching the team members in the deployment of the plan. This investment by leadership was borne out in the results. The action plan proposed by the Kaizen in Cell 1 was 94% implemented and in Cell 2 was 81% implemented after the first year of action plan implementation. A small percentage of the actions from each Kaizen were filtered out by the teams on the grounds of technical feasibility, which were in the end not implemented.

Table 2.7 presents the implementation results for the Kaizens developed in Cell 1 and Cell 2.

The L&GBM pilot testing was deemed to be successful. Overall, the pilot testing represented a significant proportion of the people and operations of the organization in Brazil. Sixty people (4% of the total workforce) and two cells (3% of the total number of cells in 2010) were involved. Therefore, the L&GBM for a cell was the right strategy for

- Improving manufacturing efficiency by optimizing the performance of its environmental flows
- Reducing manufacturing processes' environmental impact, by reducing all environmental wastes generated by production—the two main objectives of the L&GBM

TABLE 2.7

Cell 1 and Cell 2 Implementation Results

	Cell 1	Cell 2
% Action plan implemented	94%	81%
Examples of improvement opportunity ideas that were identified during the Kaizen events and that were implemented	*For reducing energy usage:* Motion sensitive and low energy lights installed in low usage areas *For reducing metallic waste generation:* Forgings were redesigned for reducing machining and hence metallic waste *For reducing contaminated waste generation:* Plastic wrap containing oil contamination was eliminated from the containers—substantial savings in disposal costs	*For reducing energy usage:* Assembly cell lighting system was replaced by a 54 W system that consumes less energy *For reducing grease waste generation:* (1) A new system was introduced to reuse the waste grease that was left in the used drums; (2) a new weighing standard was introduced in order to reduce the process waste grease
% Cost savings by reducing cell's mass and energy flows	13% After implementing the action plans (1 year)	3% After implementing the action plans (1 year)
Cost savings in US$	$132,000 Results after implementing the action plans	$15,000 Results after implementing the action plans

Source: Pampanelli, A., L&GBM, PhD Thesis, School of Engineering, UFRGS, Porto Alegre, Brazil, 2013.

The pilots proved the business case for the L&GBM and it confirmed the proposed characteristics and prerequisites. The L&GBM was then rolled out to other manufacturing cells, including sister cells (cells with the same parts and processes) and also for a value stream, which will be discussed in the next session.

Rollout the L&GBM for a Cell

The rollout of the L&GBM for a cell presented in this project was developed in GKN Driveline Operations in Brazil, during 2011 and 2012. All seven Kaizens were conducted during 2011 and the implementation of the action plans was monitored throughout 2012 and completed in December 2012. The main objectives of the rollout were as follows:

1. Applying the L&GBM in several different manufacturing cells of one manufacturing business, integrating it with preexisting Lean structure and evaluating its potential for
   a. Improving manufacturing resource utilization
   b. Reducing manufacturing processes environmental impact
2. Confirming the prerequisites by testing the model in different circumstances
3. Evaluating potential savings in terms of environmental improvements and cost reduction after applying the model
4. Identifying model improvement opportunities

The model applied for the rollout was the same as discussed earlier. The Kaizens followed the same structure presented previously, involving about 20–30 people in each of them, including operators, specialists, and managers—a diagonal slice through the organization. The agenda for the Kaizen event was the same as developed for the pilot testing, presented in Table 2.4. The data was collected accordingly to the structure given in section "Pilot Testing—L&GBM for a Cell," where the pilot test was presented. In total, seven Kaizens were conducted during 2011.

- February 2011—Cell 3
- March 2011—Cell 4
- July 2011—Cells 5, 6, and 7
- August 2011—Cells 8 and 9

The team involved in the rollout was a representative sample of the people and operations in the Brazilian factories, a total of 15% of the total workforce and 12% of the total number of cells in 2011. Involving this number of people achieved a tipping point for the site—a critical mass to achieve a change velocity for the concept. The result was that more people wanted to be involved with the L&GBM Kaizens at the site and, as a consequence, the rollout had to be controlled to avoid running away rather than being pushed.

All of the seven manufacturing cells from operations in Brazil have different characteristics in terms of prerequisites for accomplishing the L&GBM for a cell. Tables 2.8 and 2.9 present the basic characteristics of the manufacturing operational cells where the L&GBM was applied.

TABLE 2.8

Cells 3, 4, 5 and 6 Environmental and Manufacturing Characteristics, including evaluation of prerequisites

Manufacturing Characteristics	Cell 3	Cell 4	Cell 5	Cell 6
Kaizen date	Feb 11	Mar 11	Jul 11	Jul 11
Location	Brazil factory 1	Brazil factory 2	Brazil factory 2	Brazil factory 1
Nature of operations	Steel machining	Steel machining	Steel machining	Precision forming
Main cell mass and energy flows	Energy Water + Effluents Chemicals/ oils Hazardous wastes Metallic wastes	Energy Water + Effluents Chemicals/oils Metallic wastes General wastes (cleaning cloths and others)	Energy Water + Chemicals/ oils + Effluents Metallic wastes Hazardous wastes	Energy Chemicals/oils Water + Effluents Metallic wastes
Energy MWh/month	155	72.1	120.7	527
Water m³/month	36.4	3.14	9.9	18.2
Effluent m³/month	54.6	6.28	10.7	24.7
Chemicals L/month	1.4	2.9	555	3600
Metallic tons/ month	26.6	17.8	38.3	26.9
Hazardous tons/ month	1.66	0	4.3	0
Rags pc/month	0	411	0	0
Analysis of Prerequisites to Successful Deployment				
Level of Lean	Deployment level	Advanced level	Deployment level	Implementation level
Process stability	90%	more than 90%	90%	less than 90%
Application of employee engagement tools	Yes	Very high	Yes	Yes
Leadership support	Yes	Very high	Yes	Yes
Environmental awareness	Yes	Yes	Yes	Yes

(Continued)

TABLE 2.8 (*Continued*)

Cells 3, 4, 5 and 6 Environmental and Manufacturing Characteristics, Including Evaluation of Prerequisites

Analysis of Prerequisites to Successful Deployment

Use of resources	High	Medium	High	Very high
Structure for data collection	Yes	Yes	Yes	Yes
Total cost of mass and energy flows (US$/year)	$775,135	$400,782	$803,145	$1,413,956
Biggest environmental impact by cost	Metallic waste	Metallic waste	Metallic waste	Energy
	63%	66%	72%	53%

Source: Pampanelli, A., L&GBM, PhD Thesis, School of Engineering, UFRGS, Porto Alegre, Brazil, 2013.

The main objective of the Kaizen events was to reduce the consumption and wastes of natural resources for the different production mass and energy flows. Each event lasted approximately 1 day and by end of the day the teams had defined a future Green state. This future state was supported by a number of improvement actions for each cell. The results of the Kaizens are shown in Table 2.10.

Tables 2.11 and 2.12 show some of the implementation results and some examples for the Kaizens developed in these seven cells of the rollout. These Kaizens were all conducted in 2011 and the implementation results of the plans were tracked through 2011 and 2012.

The L&GBM for a cell rollout was considered successful and the mass and energy flow improvements were all monitored in 2012 and validated. Overall, after the first year of implementation, approximately 60% of the action plans for the seven Kaizens developed were implemented, saving around US$419,646, representing a 5.5% reduction of environmental cost for the cells' mass and energy flows.

The L&GBM for a cell rollout confirmed the results already presented in the pilot testing. The model can be considered a good strategy for

1. Improving manufacturing processes resources productivity by optimizing its supporting flows performance (materials and energy consumption and wastes generation)
2. Reducing manufacturing processes environmental impact, by reducing all environmental wastes generated by production

TABLE 2.9

Cells 7, 8, and 9 Environmental and Manufacturing Characteristics, Including Evaluation of Prerequisites

Manufacturing Characteristics	Cell 7	Cell 8	Cell 9
Kaizen date	Jul 11	Aug 11	Aug 11
Location	Brazil factory 2	Brazil factory 1	Brazil factory 2
Nature of operations	Steel machining	Precision forming	Steel machining
Main cell mass and energy flows	Energy	Energy	Energy
	Chemicals/oils	Chemicals/oils	Effluents
	Metallic wastes	Water + Effluents	Chemicals/oils
	Hazardous wastes	Metallic wastes	Metallic wastes
			Hazardous wastes
			General wastes
Energy consumption (MWh/month)	121	738	71.8
Chemical use (L/month)	2.3	31.1	1.6
Metallic wastes (ton/month)	18.3	27	1.5
Hazardous wastes (m^3/month)	4.4	0	4.6
Water consumption (m^3/month)	0	1.4	0
Effluent generation (m^3/month)	0	823.5	8.8
General waste unit/month	0	0	23
Analysis of Prerequisites to Successful Deployment			
Level of Lean	Deployment level	Implementing level	Deployment level
Process stability	90%	less than 90%	90%
Application of employee engagement tools	Yes	Yes	Yes
Leadership support	Yes	Yes	Yes
Environmental awareness	Yes	Yes	Yes
Use of resources	High	Very high	Low
Structure for data collection	Yes	Yes	Yes
Total cost of mass and energy flows (US$/year)	$765,272	$2,754,232	$163,032
Biggest environmental impact by cost	Metallic waste 71%	Chemicals—40% Energy—38%	Energy 62%

Source: Pampanelli, A., L&GBM, PhD Thesis, School of Engineering, UFRGS, Porto Alegre, Brazil, 2013.

TABLE 2.10

Results of the Seven Kaizen Events Developed during 2011

	Cell 3	Cell 4	Cell 5	Cell 6	Cell 7	Cell 8	Cell 9
Energy saving: (%)	2.8%	14%	10%	2%	11%	1.7%	4.7%
Water consumption reduction: (%)	100%	28%	44.8% (water, chemical, and effluents)	1.1%	NA	72%	NA
General chemical products consumption reduction: (%)	29% (oils)	86% (oils)		49% (forging oil)	60% (oils)	7.0%	76% (oils)
Effluent generation reduction: (%)	100%[a]	28%		1.1%	NA	72% (phosphate effluent)	0%
Metallic Waste generation reduction: (%)	20%	19%	1.5%	27%	1.2%	14%	0%
Hazardous waste generation reduction: (%)	55%	NA	50%	NA	50%	NA	50%
General waste generation reduction: (%)	NA	66% (cleaning cloths usage)	NA	NA	NA	NA	5.0%
Average resources reduction: (%)	50%	40%	27%	17%	31%	34%	34%

Source: Pampanelli, A., L&GBM, PhD Thesis, School of Engineering, UFRGS, Porto Alegre, Brazil, 2013.

NA, not applicable.

[a] 100% waste elimination due dry turning (air cooling of running vs. use of coolant).

TABLE 2.11

Cell 3, 4, 5 and 6 Kaizens Implementation Results

Implementation Results	Cell 3	Cell 4	Cell 5	Cell 6
% Action plan implemented (2011–2012)	68%	86%	40%	55%
Examples of improvement opportunity ideas that were identified during the Kaizen events that were implemented				
Energy use	(1) Lighting system was replaced by 54 W system that consumes less energy; (2) reduction of compressed air leakage		Implementation of a system for turning off the machines at the end of the cycle	
Chemical use	(1) Leakage elimination; (2) elimination of sources of contamination of hydraulic and cutting oils	(1) Development of containers for reusing oils in the cell; (2) implementing dry turning (air cooling) in most of operations	Reduction of the use of fluorescent concentrate due to an improvement in the mixing of the product	Daily inspection of hydraulic system to eliminate contamination of Lubrodal emulsion with hydraulic oil
Metallic waste		Reduction of extra metallic material in the part (reduction of extra material in the top of the part and through a reduction of the internal diameter)		(1) Improvement in the storage of the steel; (2) Improvement in the weighing system after the cutting operation
Water use and effluent generation	Elimination of the usage of soluble oil GROB 1146			

(Continued)

TABLE 2.11 (*Continued*)

Cell 3, 4, 5, and 6 Kaizens Implementation Results

Implementation Results	Cell 3	Cell 4	Cell 5	Cell 6
Cost saving (US$/ year) actions implemented along 2011–2012	$48,659	$76,802	$33,286	$158,973
% Cost savings by reducing cell's mass and energy flows	6.3%	19%	4%	11%

Source: Pampanelli, A., L&GBM, PhD Thesis, School of Engineering, UFRGS, Porto Alegre, Brazil, 2013.

L&GBM FOR SISTER CELLS

Sister cells are production cells that produce the same product, have the same characteristics, the same number of machines, the same type of machines, and the same number of operations. In high intense manufacturing sites, like automotive, this type of configuration is quite common. For example, it is possible to have in an assembly site, 20 cells, all similar, all them assembling the same type of components and consequently using similar amounts of raw materials and energy and generating similar quantities of wastes.

The L&GBM for sister cells is a simpler version of the L&GBM for cells. It was created as an improvement step of the L&GBM for a cell. Manufacturing organizations are always seeking for better results and improvements, adapting good ideas to maximize as much as possible the use of resources. Understanding that people involvement in Lean thinking organizations is a key element for sustaining results, the idea here was to create and test a simpler version of the L&GBM for a cell, with less steps and complexity, to replicate the improvement opportunities already identified in a previous Kaizen event, without losing the team involvement and commitment part.

Following the prerequisites presented in section "L&GBM for a Cell," for L&GBM for a cell, the prerequisites for applying the L&BM for sister cells are as follows:

1. Meet the seven prerequisites for the L&GBM for a cell.
2. Have a sister cell that has applied the L&GBM in full for a cell within the last 6 months before the proposed new Kaizen.

TABLE 2.12

Cell 7, 8, and 9 Kaizens Implementation Results

Implementation Results	Cell 7	Cell 8	Cell 9
% Action plan implemented (2011–2012)	60%	58%	50%
Examples of improvement opportunity ideas that were identified during the Kaizen events that were implemented			
Hazardous waste	Implementation of a system to reuse gridding sludge paper filter		Implementation of a system to reuse gridding sludge paper filter
Chemical products use	Improvement of machine seals to avoid oil leakages, adaptation of the system to return extra oil to the machine tanks		Changing the system that segregates gridding sludge and oil for reuse
Metallic waste		Reduction of the size/ dimension of the part)	
Water use and effluent generation		Elimination of extra sources of water entering in the phosphate line, reducing overall effluent generation	
Cost saving (US$/ year) actions implemented along 2011–2012	$30,955	$58,430	$12,539
% Cost savings by reducing cell's mass and energy flows	4%	2%	8%

Source: Pampanelli, A., L&GBM, PhD Thesis, School of Engineering, UFRGS, Porto Alegre, Brazil, 2013.

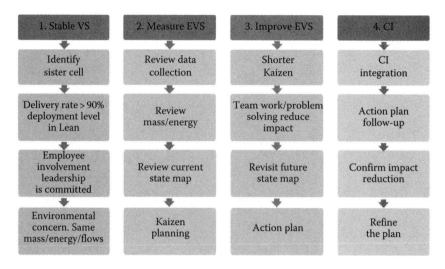

FIGURE 2.15
Four steps L&GBM for rollout to sister cells. (From Pampanelli, A., L&GBM, PhD Thesis, School of Engineering, UFRGS, Porto Alegre, Brazil, 2013.)

Figure 2.15 presents the four steps of L&GBM for sister cells, a simplified version of the L&GBM for a cell.

The overall objective of each step is described as follows:

Step 1—Identify stable value stream (VS) and environmental aspects and impacts (E): Identify an operational cell that meets all prerequisites for the L&GBM for sister cells certifying that the cell has similar type of mass and energy flows.

Step 2—Measure environmental value streams (EVS): Review the "as-is" process map or current process for the sister cell; review data collection based on the previous work (review if there are any issues in the environmental data collected for the similar cell and therefore those data can be replicated).

Step 3—Improve environmental value streams (EVS): Shorter Kaizen workshop; the objective is to review with the cell operators the previous improvement opportunities identified by the colleagues to see if these ideas will work in a similar cell and can be applied iteratively to their cell as well as generate other improvement ideas. As the specialists had already participated in the full Kaizen, the target audience for engagement were the cell operators of the sister cell. The Kaizen event for the L&GBM for a sister cell involved fewer people and required less time. Figure 2.16 presents the different group of people that were involved in the Kaizen initiative.

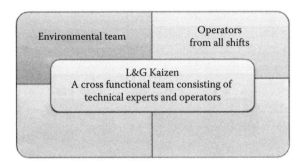

FIGURE 2.16
Groups of people that are involved in the Kaizen initiative—for a sister cell. (From Pampanelli, A., L&GBM, PhD Thesis, School of Engineering, UFRGS, Porto Alegre, Brazil, 2013.)

The basic Kaizen structure applied by the L&GBM for a sister cell includes the following:

- *Phase 1:* About half hour for introduction, understanding the actual state, the costs, and the environmental impacts of the cell mass and energy flows.
- *Phase 2:* About 1 h for team workshop floor exercise. The objective of this is to understand the flow of use or generation of such resource during each cell operation and to verify if the ideas identified in the full Kaizen by the other colleagues can be validated here.
- *Phase 3:* About 1 h for consolidating a new action plan for the cell, replicating the previous ideas identified during the full Kaizen event and adding new ones.

Step 4—Continuous improvement (CI): Develop action and communication plans in the Kaizen workshop. Sustainability of the results achieved in the Kaizen through leadership standard work.

Applying the L&GBM to Sister Cells

The rollout of the L&GBM for sister cells presented in this project was developed during 2011. The implementations of the action plans were monitored in 2012 and were finalized in December 2012. The objectives of the testing were

1. Applying and testing the L&GBM for sisters in several different manufacturing cells of one manufacturing business
2. Confirming the prerequisites

3. Evaluating potential savings in terms of environmental improvements and cost reduction after applying the model and comparing it with the L&GBM for a cell
4. Identifying model improvement opportunities

In total, 3 Kaizens were developed during 2011, involving 10 sister cells, according to the agenda presented in the following:

- August 2011—Cells 4.1 and 4.2 sister cells to Cell 4
- September 2011—Cells 9.1, 9.2, 9.3, and 9.4, sister cells to Cell 9
- November 2011—Cells 9.5, 9.6, 9.7, 9.8, sister cells to Cell 9

Table 2.13 presents the basic characteristics of the manufacturing operational cells where the L&GBM for sister cells was applied.

After 3 h of carrying out the Kaizen event, with the objective of reducing cost, waste, and consumption in natural resources for different production mass and energy flows (energy, metallic waste, chemical products, hazards waste, effluents, and water), the teams that were participating in each event defined a new future state for the cells, identifying improvement opportunities for each one of the cell supporting flows.

Table 2.14 presents the implementation results for the three Kaizens. These Kaizens were all developed during 2011 and the implementation results of the plans were tracked through 2011 and 2012.

The mass and energy flow improvements, as a result of the L&GBM for sister cells, were all monitored during 2012 and the improved results were all confirmed. Overall, after a year of implementation, approximately 32% of the action plans for the three Kaizens developed were implemented, saving approximately US$28,843, which represented 1.7% reduction for the cells mass and energy flows.

Although the idea of the L&GBM for sister cells was to develop a simpler Kaizen, results show that the insufficient involvement of the environmental specialists and their subsequent analysis of the mass and energy flows during the Kaizens resulted in the action plans being implemented to a lesser degree (32% in this case, whereas for the rollout, the average level of action plan implementation was 60%), and, as a consequence, a reduction in both mass and energy flow savings (1.7% in this case, for the rollout the average was 5.5%).

TABLE 2.13

Environmental and manufacturing characteristics of the cells where the L&GBM for Sisters Cells was applied, including the application and evaluation of the cell prerequisites

Manufacturing Characteristics	Cells 4.1_4.2	Cells 9.1_9.2_9.3_9.4	Cells 9.5_9.6_9.7_9.8
Kaizen date	Aug 11	Sep 11	Nov 11
Location	Brazil factory 2	Brazil factory 2	Brazil factory 2
Nature of operations	Steel machining	Steel machining	Steel machining
Main Cell—Mass and Energy Flow			
Energy	Yes	Yes	Yes
Water and effluents	Yes	Yes	Yes
Chemicals and oils	No	Yes	Yes
Metallic wastes	Yes	Yes	Yes
General wastes	Yes	Yes	Yes
Hazardous wastes	No	Yes	Yes
Energy Mw/h	186	287	287
Water m³/month	1.3	35.2	35.2
Chemicals L/month	58	6.5	6.5
Metallic waste t/month	35.4	5.8	5.8
Hazardous waste m³/month	NA	18.4	18.4
General waste	NA	92	92
Analysis of Prerequisites			
Level of Lean	Advanced level	Deployment level	Deployment level
Process stability	more than 90%	less than 90%	less than 90%
Application of employee engagement tools	Very high	In place	In place
Leadership support	Very high	In place	In place
Environmental awareness	In place	In place	In place
Use of resources	Medium	Low	Low
Structure for data collection	In place	In place	In place
Total cost of mass and energy flows (US$/year)	$592,710	$652,129	$670,129
Major impact in the cell environmental cost	Metallic waste 66%	Energy 62%	Energy 62%

Source: Pampanelli, A., L&GBM, PhD Thesis, School of Engineering, UFRGS, Porto Alegre, Brazil, 2013.

TABLE 2.14

Cells 4.1_4.2, Cells 9.1_9.2_9.3_9.4, and Cells 9.5_9.6_9.7_9.8 Kaizens Implementation Results

Implementation Results	Cells 4.1_4.2	Cells 9.1_9.2_9.3_9.4	Cells 9.5_9.6_9.7_9.8
% Action plan implemented (2011–2012)	65%	14%	18%
Examples of improvement opportunity ideas that were identified during the Kaizen events that were implemented	*For reducing chemical products usage:* Development of recipients for reusing oils in the cell *For reducing water consumption and effluent generation:* Reuse water from washing machine and air conditioners for cleaning floors	*For reducing chemical products usage:* Elimination of chemical products leakages	*For reducing energy usage:* Lighting system was replaced by a 54 W system that consumes less energy *For reducing water consumption and effluent generation:* Reuse water from air conditioners for cleaning the floors
Cost saving (US$/year) actions implemented along 2011–2012	$21,047	$3,147	$4,648
% Cost savings by reducing cell's mass and energy flows	3.5% After implementing the action plans	0.5% After implementing the action plans	1% After implementing the action plans

Source: Pampanelli, A., L&GBM, PhD Thesis, School of Engineering, UFRGS, Porto Alegre, Brazil, 2013.

L&GBM FOR A VALUE STREAM

As described previously, value streams are the flow of material and information across multiple processes, so that individual process-level improvement efforts fit together as a flowing value stream, match the organization's objectives, and serve the requirements of external customers. In order to manage by Lean thinking principles, most Lean thinking organizations use value stream mapping. Value stream mapping is a Lean manufacturing technique used to analyze and design the flow of materials and information required to bring a product or service to a customer or consumer. At Toyota, where the technique was originated, it is known as "material and information flow mapping." It can be applied to nearly any value chain. Although value stream mapping is often associated with manufacturing, it is also used in logistics, supply chain, service-related industries, health care, software development, and product development.

The same idea of redesigning a value stream for improving flow is applied by the L&GBM to a value stream. The difference here is the focus. While traditional value stream application will be focused in fulfilling the client's need, the one that buys or requests a finished good or a service, L&GBM will be focused also on preserving the environment. Therefore, the objective here will be to reduce environmental impact and improve the use of resources. As in the cell model, the objects of study in the L&GBM for a value stream will be the supporting environmental flows for production, mass and energy consumption, and wastes generation. There is an important difference to be considered here, because the end customer for L&GBM for a value stream is the environment. This difference will be explained along the following paragraphs.

From a manufacturing perspective, one factory or one location may have more than one product or product family being produced. As a consequence, it may have more than one value stream, all of them coexisting in the same physical location. This is fine for a Lean organization since it will mean that in this case the value stream analysis will need to be developed individually, by value stream, as well as through the implementation of improvement opportunities. A value stream map generally defines the Lean boundary. Lean promotes high efficiency within the boundary of the system as defined by a value stream map intent on minimizing non–value added. Lean promotes resource conservation inside that boundary, which may be the walls of a plant or may extend to supply chains. The Lean path conserves resources in an environmental sense—fewer and shorter material moves, compacting space, and improving process—they waste less material or energy doing things that really did not need to be done.

Sustainability goes beyond this to include environmental impact. So, this very same approach cannot be applicable when the focus is the environment. As discussed in Chapter 1, Green thinking sees waste as extraction and consequential disposal of resources at rates or in forms beyond that which nature can absorb. Nature is symbiotic. The environmental impact of a production process is dependent on the surrounding environment, the soil, the air, etc. Several value streams coexisting in the same location, same site, and same physical place may have a completely

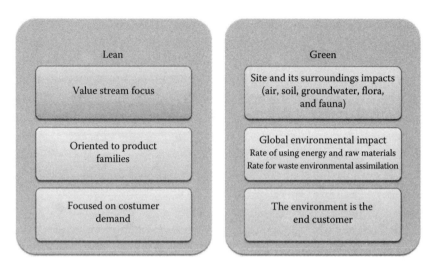

FIGURE 2.17

The L&GBM analysis of a value stream—in order to cope with the environmental principles the model considers all the value streams that compose one physical location. (From Pampanelli, A., L&GBM, PhD Thesis, School of Engineering, UFRGS, Porto Alegre, Brazil, 2013.)

different impact (systemic and synergetic) on the surrounding environment than their individual impact. Figure 2.17 presents a framework to express this idea.

The difference between an original value stream analysis of a product and the overall site mass and energy balances applied by the L&GBM illustrate this difference in thinking. If several value streams coexist in the same physical place, this is fine from an end customer point of view. In the case of the environment that is synergic and dependent on the surrounding environmental conditions, the L&GBM for a value stream proposes the analysis of them all together, and thus considering the overall environmental impact for one specific site. This means that the mass and energy analysis of a value stream, one site, will not be divided by product families, but it will be focused in analysis of the overall impact to the end customer of this process, which is the environment. The expected output of the L&GBM for a value stream is the degree of improvement in these flows and it will be focused in establishing strategies for

1. Producing with the maximum productivity in the use of natural resources
2. Minimum environmental impact

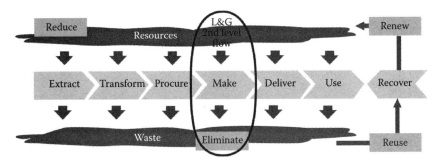

FIGURE 2.18
Boundaries of the L&GBM to a value stream. (From Pampanelli, A., L&GBM, PhD Thesis, School of Engineering, UFRGS, Porto Alegre, Brazil, 2013.)

But it will not be analyzing mass and energy flows of a factory oriented by product families. L&GBM to a value stream will be analyzing mass and energy flows of a factory having the environment as the end customer and hence considering the analysis of its overall impact. Besides that difference, all the other characteristics of the L&GBM for a value stream are quite similar to the model presented for the cell, the first level flow. The L&GBM to a value stream is applied to the second level flow for the production step of the extended value stream including all the value streams that coexist in one manufacturing site and their surrounding impact on the environment. Figure 2.18 presents this idea.

Following is a description of the main prerequisites considered necessary for a factory/value stream to be eligible for applying the L&GBM:

1. An overall stable process across all value streams, with delivery records over 90%
2. A mature deployment level in using and applying Lean tools—for all value streams within the site
3. EI systems in place—managers already know and apply the most common employee involvement (EI) tools for team involvement, such as daily meetings, primary visual display, weekly meetings, recognition, etc.
4. Supportive management team
5. Factory is ISO 14001 certified and it is on its second improvement cycle
6. Factory has a significant use of resources (materials, chemicals, water, waste, effluent, and energy)
7. Structure in place for environmental data collection

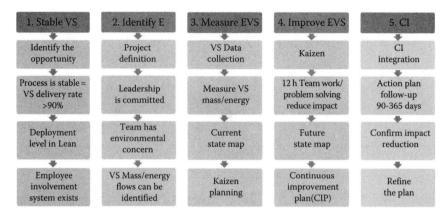

FIGURE 2.19

Five steps L&GBM for improving supporting flows performance in a factory. (From Pampanelli, A., L&GBM, PhD Thesis, School of Engineering, UFRGS, Porto Alegre, Brazil, 2013.)

Figure 2.19 represents the basic standard framework for L&GBM to a value stream.

The key objective of each step is described as follows:

Step 1—Stable value stream (VS): Identify the need for improvement. Identify a site that has the prerequisites of the L&GBM for a value stream.

Step 2—Identify environmental aspects and impacts (E): Define the process improvement scope by identifying the environmental aspects and impacts of the value stream (in this case, the factory). Aspect and impact definitions are considered according to ISO 14001:2004 (ISO, 2004). An environmental aspect is a feature, or characteristic, of an activity, product, or service that affects or can affect the environment, the cell inputs or the cell outputs. An environmental impact is a change to the environment caused by environmental aspects resulting from cell inputs, and outputs.

Step 3—Measure environmental value streams (EVS): Identify the actual data on the environmental process. Collect environmental data. Map "as-is," or current process and identify the environmental process actual data for the whole site, analyzing the overall productivity in the use of resources and the site potential impact on the environment. Organize the Kaizen event. Draw the project scope and align the objectives for the improvement with the site plant manager and executive team. Define a list of people to be involved, since this will require the involvement of several managers and specialists.

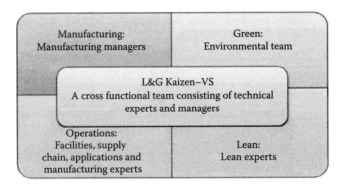

FIGURE 2.20
Groups of people that are involved in the Kaizen initiative—for a VS. (From Pampanelli, A., L&GBM, PhD Thesis, School of Engineering, UFRGS, Porto Alegre, Brazil, 2013.)

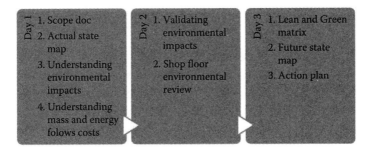

FIGURE 2.21
L&GBM to a value stream—Kaizen structure. (From Pampanelli, A., L&GBM, PhD Thesis, School of Engineering, UFRGS, Porto Alegre, Brazil, 2013.)

Step 4—Improve environmental value streams (EVS): Identify waste elimination opportunities during a Kaizen workshop. Figure 2.20 presents the people that are involved in the Kaizen initiative.

Figure 2.21 presents the basic structure for the Kaizen event applied by the L&GBM to a value stream.

- *Day 1:* About 3 h for introduction, understanding the actual state, the costs, and the environmental impacts of the factory mass and energy flows and for organizing the cross-functional teams that will be responsible for each one of the supporting flows (energy, waste, water, chemicals, etc.).
- *Day 2:* Around 6 h for team workshop floor exercise. The objective of each team is to understand the flow of use or generation of such resource during operation and its environmental impact. For this, the aspects and impact evaluation sheets from ISO 14001 are used.

At the end of the exercise, a prioritization matrix is completed and it is possible to identify the production supporting flows that have more environmental impact as well as the parts, stages, and cells that are responsible for the greatest resources usage and waste generation.

- *Day 3:* Around 3 h for consolidating the future state map for the mass and energy flows and action plan for the improvement opportunities as well as for prioritizing the cells that represent the greatest environmental impact and where the L&GBM for a cell should be applied (systemic approach). Map the "to-be," or future process, considering all the analysis developed and create the future map for the supporting production flows studied during the Kaizen.

Step 5—Continuous improvement (CI): Develop action and communication plans in the Kaizen workshop. Ensure sustainability of the results achieved in the Kaizen through leadership standard work (LSW—leader's standard work or leadership validation): Validate the action plan with the leadership; establish a connection between the action plan and the environmental management system (ISO 14001) objectives and targets.

Figures 2.22 and 2.23 present the frameworks of what is to be expected after applying the L&GBM to a value stream. Applying the L&GBM for a value

Identification of mass and energy flows	Productivity in the use of natural resources and impact reduction	Continuous improvement 2–3 years cycle
Energy		Year 1 Priorization of mass and energy flow
Raw material, raw material wastes		Environmental strategic projects review Identification of 1st level flow Kaizens
Water, chemicals, effluents	Second level flow Kaizen event	Year 2 Environmental performance evaluation Project stage review
Oils, waste oils		Cost savings review Lessons learned
Contaminated wastes		Year 3 Priorization of mass and energy flow Environmental strategic projects review Identification of 1st level flow Kaizens
	Employee involvement	3–5 years environment continuous improvement plan
	Problem solving	Strategic sustainability plan for the main mass and energy flows

FIGURE 2.22

L&GBM to a value stream 2–3 year improvement cycle structure. (From Pampanelli, A., L&GBM, PhD Thesis, School of Engineering, UFRGS, Porto Alegre, Brazil, 2013.)

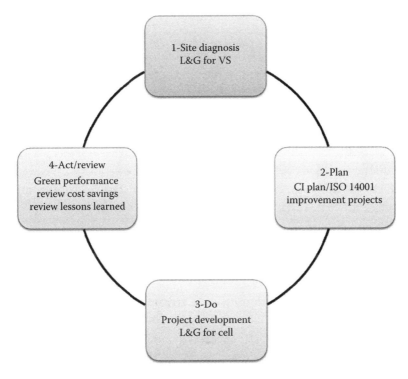

FIGURE 2.23
L&GBM to a value stream final planning integrated to the site EMS (ISO 14001) system. (From Pampanelli, A., L&GBM, PhD Thesis, School of Engineering, UFRGS, Porto Alegre, Brazil, 2013.)

stream, the overall factory environmental performance needs to be reviewed to fully understand the impact on the environment. The main benefits are achieved by completely integrating the L&GMB analysis and improvement opportunities with factory environmental management structure. Since the projects identified in the value stream level require engineering, analysis, and planning, the L&GBM initiative should be integrated to the business management structure, as part of a 2- to 3-year improvement cycle.

Following this, the L&GBM initiative will be a key step in this process for establishing the site environmental diagnosis. The heart of the model is the identification of the process flows for the main environmental impacts, developed during the Kaizen event. The improvement opportunities identified in the Kaizen initiative should be integrated to the site continuous improvement plan and ISO 140001/EMS plans. The continuous improvement is sustained through management review of critical value streams and deployment of environmental continuous improvement plans (CIP) for business strategic projects. The development of the improvement projects and the Kaizens at the cell level will compose the operational building block of this cycle that will terminate, in every established period, in reviewing of overall environmental performance, cost savings, and lessons learned by the period.

Applying the L&GBM to a Value Stream

The application of the L&GBM to a value stream was launched in the operations in Brazil, across two sites in November 22, 2011. The action plan was tracked during 2012 and the second level flow Kaizen event was repeated on November 28, 2012.

The main objectives of this test were as follows:

1. Identifying and confirming the prerequisites for L&GBM applied to a manufacturing value stream
2. Using the L&GBM for a value stream to prioritize subsequent L&GBM first level of flow Kaizens for 2012
3. Understanding mass and energy second level flow current state and identifying improvement opportunities through team work, proposing a new future state and an action plan
4. Integrating L&GBM for a value stream within the existing site planning and improvement structure

The structure used for applying the L&GBM for a value stream was the same presented in section "L&GBM for a Value Stream." Figure 2.24 presents the Kaizen scope.

All the data used for the Kaizen event was collected, compiled, and organized by the Brazil Environmental Team (environmental specialists). This preparation was key to the success of the Kaizen. It enabled the event to focus on the future state and actions rather than spend frustrating time stalling the Kaizen to collect data. The data used for this Kaizen have the following sources:

- *Energy:* Energy meters were used for collecting energy data (this was accomplished through the site's metering system, energy suppliers' meters, and site internet energy system). Data was collected for the factory sites on a monthly basis. Energy invoices were used to assess the cost accurately.
- *Water:* Water meters were used for collecting water data (site metering system, water suppliers' meters, and site internet system).

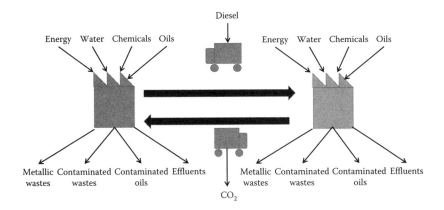

FIGURE 2.24
Brazil operations: mass and energy flows that were studied during the Kaizens. (Adapted from Pampanelli, A., L&GBM, PhD Thesis, School of Engineering, UFRGS, Porto Alegre, Brazil, 2013.)

Data was collected for the factory sites on a monthly basis. Water invoices were used to assess the costs accurately.

- *Metallic and contaminated wastes:* Every single container of waste generated by factory sites was weighed before they left the sites. The site weighing system was used and an internet system was used for processing monthly waste generation data. Waste invoices were used to assess the cost.
- *Oils and chemicals:* The site ERP material system was used to access the consumption of each individual source of chemical used by the factory sites. Invoices were used to access the cost.
- *Effluents:* Effluent meters were used for collecting data for each individual stream of effluent generated by the factory sites on a monthly basis. Invoices for chemicals and environmental waste were used to access the cost of the effluent generated by the sites.

As shown in Figure 2.24, at the value stream level, the data used is the result of all the Brazilian operations' mass and energy flows. The data used for the Kaizens in this case are site level data. The metering system used for collecting the data is maintained and calibrated according with site measurement system standards (ISO 14001:2004/Clause 4.5.1—monitoring and measuring). The source of data used for the Kaizen is the same one that the factory uses for submitting information to external authorities. It is inspected annually by external auditors for certification of accuracy and confidence of the measurement.

The second level flow Kaizens developed in Brazil followed the same structure presented in section "L&GBM for a Value Stream," involving about 30 people in a cross functional team consisting of technical experts and managers.

As mentioned in section "L&GBM for a Value Stream," the concept of L&GBM for a value stream is that the improvement opportunities will be integrated as part of the continuous improvement structure of the site. The agenda and Kaizen structure was based on this idea, as presented previously in Figure 2.21.

In the case of operations in Brazil, it was developed in years 1 and 2 of the 2–3 years improvement cycle proposed by the L&GBM for a value stream.

The second level flow (VSM) Kaizen was first developed during November 2011. In that year, the results for the mass and energy flows of the value stream were reviewed, environmental strategic projects were identified, and the first level flow Kaizens were prioritized. With the action plan identified, improvement opportunities were implemented and results were tracked during 2012.

Data was then collected again and a new Kaizen conducted in 2012. In this new Kaizen, the results were reviewed, (environmental performance review), projects and cost savings were analyzed, and lessons from the Kaizen captured. A new improvement plan was generated for the 2013 period. This process is detailed in the following pages.

Table 2.15 presents the basic characteristics of operations in Brazil, including the evaluation L&GBM for value stream prerequisites for the Kaizens developed in 2011 and 2012.

Table 2.16 presents 2011 data and results for the mass and energy flows studied for the application of the L&GBM for the value stream for Brazil manufacturing operations.

During the first Kaizen, in 2011, all managers and specialists participating in the Kaizen were invited to review the actual state, analyze improvement opportunities, and propose a future state. For developing this activity, managers and specialists were divided into teams and they followed the agenda proposed in Figure 2.21, including

- Day 1—3 h for reviewing the project scope and understand actual state
- Day 2—3 h for setting a common overview about manufacturing areas, main environmental impacts, and costs rate
- Day 3—3 h for creating the action plan and prioritize the high-impact easy to do

TABLE 2.15

L&GBM for VS—Project Scope and Analysis of Prerequisites

Lean and Green Kaizen Project Scope

GKN site name	Brazil—sites 1 and 2
Main products	Precision forming parts, components, and half-shafts
Nature of operations	(1) Machining
	(2) Painting
	(3) Heat treatment
	(4) Assembly
	(5) Precision forming
	(6) Phosphate treatment of forged parts
Activities included in the value stream analysis	(1) Machining
	(4) Assembly
	(5) Precision forming
	(6) Phosphate treatment
Activities excluded of the value stream analysis	(2) Painting
	(3) Heat treatment
	These two processes were excluded because they are two unique cells, therefore, they will be treated separately, as for level 1 flow Kaizens

Lean and Green Kaizen—Prerequisites

Year	2011	2012
Dates of the Kaizens	November 22, 2011	November 29, 2012
Sales in the period	6,200,000 SEH	6,400,000 Half-shafts
Annual tones of shipped parts	57197 ton	59038 ton
Average customer delivery rating	92%	94%
Level of Lean	Deployment	Deployment
Application of employee engagement tools	Deployment	Deployment
Cell/site ISO 14001 certification	Since 2000–4° cycle	Since 2000–4° cycle
Data of the latest environmental training received by the site team members	July 2011	June 2012
Does the site have an intense use of resources?	Yes	Yes
Are the main supporting e-flows are cost intensive?	Yes	Yes
Data collection structure in place for environmental flows?	Yes	Yes

Source: Pampanelli, A., L&GBM, PhD Thesis, School of Engineering, UFRGS, Porto Alegre, Brazil, 2013.

TABLE 2.16

Data Collected for Mass and Energy Flows—2011 Period

	Electric Energy	Metallic Wastes	Water, Machining Chemicals, and Effluents	Oils and Contaminated Oils	Contaminated Wastes
Main supporting flows description	Electric energy	Metallic wastes (chips) Scrap (piercing, bars, and others) Metallic sludge	Water effluents Cooling liquids	Oils (for machines, maintenance, and protection) Waste oils	Contaminated filter paper Contaminated grease Contaminated boots General contaminated wastes (plastic, paper, and others)
E-flows— physical measurement	86.185 MWh	12.739 ton	*Water:* 112,467 m³ *Effluents:* Shaft: 2310 m³ Phosphate: 7798 m³ PF: 1445 m³ POA: 6675 m³ Cooling liquids Shaft: 15 320 L Phosphate: 51 695 L PF: 357 510 L POA: 93 556 L	*Oils:* 730630 L *Waste oils:* 105640 L	*Total contaminated waste:* *1640 m³ +* *35,610 pieces of rubber*
Actual state cost results ($)	$9.77 m	$22.41 m	$3.63 m	$1.87 m	$0.69 m
Environmental performance indicators: (e-flow/tons of parts)	1.506 Mhw/ ton	0.222 ton/ ton	1.966 m³ water/ton 0.2 m³ effluent POA/ton	12.77 L new oil/ton	0.028 m³/ton

Source: Pampanelli, A., L&GBM, PhD Thesis, School of Engineering, UFRGS, Porto Alegre, Brazil, 2013.

	Electrical energy	Metallic waste	Water, chemical, and effluents	Oils and contaminated oils	Contaminated wastes
Cell 1					
Usage	H	H	H	M	M
$ Cost	H	H	H	L	L
Production critically	H	L	H	L	H
Overall	**H**	**H**	**H**	**M**	**M**
Cell 2					
Usage	L	H	L	L	H
$ Cost	H	H	L	L	H
Production critically	L	L	L	L	L
Overall	**M**	**H**	**L**	**L**	**H**

FIGURE 2.25
Example of shop floor environmental review developed during the Kaizen. (Adapted from Pampanelli, A., L&GBM, PhD Thesis, School of Engineering, UFRGS, Porto Alegre, Brazil, 2013.)

The operations at the sites in Brazil have six operational manufacturing units, each led by one manufacturing manager. The teams reviewed all operations and processes in order to identify the key points for environmental impact, cost impact, and flow impact. Figure 2.25 presents an example of the exercise developed with the team while they were on the shop floor.

The teams took 6 h to accomplish this stage, three in Site 1 and three in Site 2. Then, on the final day, the team was divided into five teams, each representing one of the five environmental flows that are being studied, with the objective of reducing cost, waste, and consumption of natural resources for different production mass and energy flows (energy, metallic waste, chemical products, hazards waste, effluents, and water). After 3 h, the teams analyzed the actual conditions and, based on the information collected during day one and day two, proposed a new future state and identified improvement opportunities for each one of the mass and energy supporting flows.

The team of managers and specialists put together an action plan for each one of the mass and energy flows studied, with a total of 41 key strategic actions to be implemented, with a potential cost saving of US$1.16 million. The proposed plan was integrated at the site ISO 14001 system

(EMS)/continuous improvement system. The plan was tracked through the entire year by the site leadership team.

The environmental managers reviewed the plan again. From the 41 actions proposed, just two were cancelled as they were not considered feasible due to their cost and minimal environmental impact, that is,

- *Metallic waste value stream:* Changing the tooling for producing precision formed parts
- *Oils value stream:* Changing the oil controlling system

From the 39 actions that were considered viable to be implemented, 8 were implemented during 2012, representing 21% of the actions identified in the original workshop. These had a direct cost saving of US$0.8 m. The actions implemented were as follows:

- Energy value stream:
  1. Changing cold water pumping system
  2. Energy reactive correction
  3. Implementing of a system for monitoring and controlling compressed air leakages
- Metallic waste value stream:
  4. Changing of parts design
- Water/chemicals value stream:
  5. Changing lubricant system
- Oils value stream:
  6. Implementing of internal oil regeneration system—with oil regeneration truck
  7. Implementing a system to reuse oil
- Waste value stream:
  8. Implementation of automatic system for reuse of waste grease

Also, based on the information collected during the shop floor exercise, the Kaizen team proposed a list of cells that should be prioritized for first level flow Kaizens since these cells represented a significant use of mass and energy. Based on this prioritization, 10 new first level flow Kaizens were developed in critical areas. These contributed significantly to the overall mass and energy flow reduction.

Together, the 10 cell Kaizens conducted during 2011 (rollout and sister cells) and 10 new Kaizens developed saved US$0.45 m.

Therefore, both strategies (implementation of second level flow improvement projects and implementation of first level flow actions) generated direct savings of US$0.8 m plus $0.45 m, totaling $1.25 m of direct and measurable L&GBM savings for the 2011/2012 periods.

In order to confirm these results, a new round of data collection for 2012 period was developed. Table 2.17 presents the 2012 data and results for the mass and energy flows of Brazil manufacturing operations.

Table 2.18 presents the comparable results of cost and environmental indicators for 2011 and 2012 periods.

As can be seen in Table 2.18, environmental performance improved in all value streams after implementing L&GBM for a value stream. The energy savings were so significant that they even offset the 20% increase in unit costs that occurred during the time of the Kaizen and the implementation of the action plans. In all the other four supporting flows, even with an increase in price, the consumption reduction was so significant that all four had significant reduction in cost.

With this second round of data collection, a second L&GBM for a VS Kaizen was conducted in November 2012, following the same structure presented in section "L&GBM for a Value Stream," involving about 30 people in a cross-functional team consisting of technical experts and managers. In this new Kaizen the results (environmental performance), projects, and cost savings were reviewed, lessons learned were raised and evaluated, and a new improvement plan was generated for the 2013 period.

The Kaizen team proposed a plan of 30 actions to be tracked by senior management during 2013, integrating to ISO 14001 system (EMS)/ continuous improvement system. Nineteen actions are new actions, identified by the team during the last VS Kaizen. Eleven actions that originated from the 2011/2012 plan were kept by the team for the 2013 period.

The application of the model also identified the three main environmental costs of Brazil operations, which are

1. Metallic
2. Energy
3. Water and chemicals

These results proved that a preventive approach in terms of improving manufacturing processes resources productivity by optimizing its supporting flows performance (materials and energy consumption) would

TABLE 2.17

Data Collected for Mass and Energy Flows—2012 Period

	Electric Energy	Metallic Wastes	Water, Machining Chemicals, and Effluents	Oils and Contaminated Oils	Contaminated Wastes
Main supporting flows description	Electric energy	Metallic wastes (chips) Scrap (piercing, bars, and others) Metallic sludge	Water Effluents Cooling liquids	Oils (for machines, maintenance, and protection) Waste oils	Contaminated filter paper Contaminated grease Contaminated boots General contaminated wastes (plastic, paper, and others)
E-flows— physical measurement	82.8 MWh	12.39 ton	*Water:* 114.410 m³ *Effluents:* Shaft: 1.749 m³ Phosphate: 7.820 m³ PF: 1.044 m³ POA: 5.120 m³ *Cooling liquids* Shaft: 15.900 L Phosphate: 39.125 L PF: 287.939 L POA: 94.710 L	*Oils:* 712.1 L *Waste oils:* 43.76 L	*Total contaminated waste:* 1.08 m³ + 42.450 pieces of boots
Actual state cost results ($)	$10.37 m	$20.76 m	$3.23 m	$1.87 m	$0.48 m
Environmental performance indicators: (e-flow/tons of parts)	1.40 Mhw/ ton	0.209 ton/ton	1.937 m³ water/ton 0.15 m³ effluent POA/ton	12.06 L new oil/ton	0.017 m³/ton

Source: Pampanelli, A., L&GBM, PhD Thesis, School of Engineering, UFRGS, Porto Alegre, Brazil, 2013.

TABLE 2.18

L&GBM for VS—Comparable Results of Cost and Environmental Indicators (US$)

	Energy	Metallic Wastes	Water and Effluents	Oils	Contaminated Wastes
2011 Cost ($)	9.77 m	22.40 m	3.63 m	1.867 m	0.695 m
2012 Cost($)	10.37 m	20.76 m	3.23 m	1.865 m	0.475 m
% Improvement	+6.1%	7.3%	11%	0.1%	32%
2011	1.506	0.222	1.966	12.77	0.028
Environmental performance	Mhw/ton	ton/ton	m³ water/ ton	L new oil/ton	m³/ton
2012 Environmental performance	1.40 Mhw/ton	0.209 ton/ton	1.937 m³ water/ ton	12.06 L new oil/ton	0.017 m³/ton
% Improvement	7%	6%	2%	6%	40%

Source: Pampanelli, A., L&GBM, PhD Thesis, School of Engineering, UFRGS, Porto Alegre, Brazil, 2013.

be a good strategy not only for reducing manufacturing processes environmental impact, but also for improving the operational financial performance.

The model also proves that integrating Green with an operational approach can make businesses more competitive. In the case of pilot company, the L&GBM initiative brought direct savings of US$1.25 m and indirect nonmeasurable savings (due the better environmental awareness and use of resources) of US$0.43 m. This means that the Brazilian plant saved US$1.68 m in this period by

1. Improving manufacturing processes resources productivity
2. Reducing manufacturing processes environmental impact. In order words, it means that the environmental cost was reduced by 4.5% in this period

Therefore, the L&GBM for a VS confirmed all the objectives planned for this testing, including confirmation of VS prerequisites, the use of the VS Kaizens to prioritize L&GBM first level of flow Kaizens, identification of improvement opportunities through team work, proposing a new future state and an action plan, and the idea of integrating L&GBM for VS with the site existing structure (strategic planning, improvement plans, and ISO 14001 System).

The model can be considered an effective strategy for

1. Improving manufacturing processes resources productivity by optimizing its supporting flows performance (materials and energy consumption and wastes generation)
2. Reducing manufacturing processes environmental impact by reducing all environmental wastes generated by production

A more detailed discussion about the model will be presented in Chapter 3.

REVERSE TESTING: APPLYING THE L&GBM TO A CELL IN DIFFERENT MANUFACTURING ENVIRONMENTS

The pilot testing presented in this part of the project is related to the full application of the L&GBM for a cell in different manufacturing environments for the following operations:

- Aerospace, United Kingdom: October 2010
- Automotive, United States: May and August 2011
- Metals, United States: May 2010

The sites participated voluntarily.

The main objectives of the pilot testing of the L&GBM for a cell in different manufacturing environments were

(1) To confirm if the five-step model proposed and structure for the L&GBM for a cell can be applied to any type of manufacturing business
(2) To confirm the prerequisites, considering different manufacturing environments
(3) To analyze potential savings in terms of environmental improvements and cost reduction after applying the model
(4) To review ways of working when applying the model in different business conditions

The pilot Kaizen events were conducted at the end of 2010 and 2011, following the five-steps model described in section "L&GBM for a Cell."

By applying the model in different types of cells with different levels of Lean deployment via cross-functional Kaizen team events ensured that all the team members were fully involved and had the opportunity to contribute their ideas.

Although the initial idea of the pilot testing was to implement the five-steps model fully in the three sites, that were not possible. All the three sites presented problems in accomplishing one or more phases of the model as presented:

- *Kaizen in aerospace:* Steps 1–4 were implemented 100%. Step 5 (implementation of the action plan) was not accomplished.
- *Kaizen in automotive systems:* Steps 1–4 were implemented 100%. Step 5 was implemented partially.
- *Kaizen in metals:* Steps 1 and 2 were implemented 100%. Steps 3–5 were not developed and therefore they do not have an action plan to be implemented.

Table 2.19 presents basic characteristics of the three manufacturing operational cells where the L&GBM for cells was planned to be tested as well as some Kaizen results for aerospace and automotive system sites.

The automotive systems Kaizen was implemented partially but the site did not provide the final figures for their achievements. For the other two Kaizens, the process is analyzed but the implementation results will not be considered, since the action plan in aerospace was not implemented and the Kaizen in metals did not even happen.

The pilot testing in other global sites generated a host of hidden issues that were not considered in the original work in Brazil. The sites were chosen through a senior level top-down process that did not consider all of the enabling prerequisites that were proven to be required in Brazil. One site was chosen due to its high-energy usage and therefore potential to save costs. However, this site was not mature in its Lean deployment and other priorities at the site meant resources were switched to support new product introduction. Another site found a similar lower level of Lean deployment; however, the key here was the absence of the local environmental expert who was unable to attend the session. This coupled with a loss of

TABLE 2.19

Environmental and Manufacturing Characteristics of the Pilot Cells Where the L&GBM for Cells was Planned to Be Tested, Including the Application and Evaluation Cell Prerequisites and Results

Manufacturing Characteristics	Aerospace	Automotive Systems	Metals
Kaizen date	October 2010	May 2011 and August 2011	May 2011
Location	UK	USA	USA
Nature of operations	Aluminum machining of parts for airplanes	Steel machining and assembly of parts for large vehicles	Heat treatment processes of parts for industrial application
Main cell mass and energy flows	Energy Chemicals/oils Aluminum wastes	Energy Water Chemicals/oils Metallic wastes General and contaminated wastes	Energy Water Endo gas Metallic wastes
Actual state data: Energy and materials consumption and wastes generation	Energy consumption: Not evaluated due to difficulties in collecting and analyzing energy data Chemicals/oils usage: 26 m³/ month Al wastes: 35 ton/ month	Data was collected properly but the site did not provide the figures	Not evaluated due to difficulties in collecting environmental data
Analysis of Prerequisites			
Level of Lean	Implementing level	Implementing level	Implementing level
Process stability	Less than 90%	90%	Less than 90%
Application of employee engagement tools	Medium	In place	Medium
Leadership support	Medium	In place	Medium
Environmental awareness	In place	In place	In place
Use of resources	Very high	Medium	High
Structure for data collection	Medium	Medium	Not in place

(*Continued*)

TABLE 2.19 (*Continued*)

Environmental and Manufacturing Characteristics of the Pilot Cells Where the L&GBM for Cells was Planned to Be Tested, Including the Application and Evaluation Cell Prerequisites and Results

Analysis of Prerequisites			
Total cost of mass and energy flows (US$/year)	$5879700	Data not available	Not evaluated
Major impact in the cell environmental cost	Aluminum waste 98%	Data not available	Not evaluated
Results of Kaizen Event			
Energy reduction (%)	Not evaluated	5%	Not evaluated
Water reduction (%)	6%	2%	Not evaluated
Chemical products consumption reduction: (%)	10% (oils)	15% (oils)	Not evaluated
Total waste generation reduction: (%)	2%	7%	Not evaluated

Source: Pampanelli, A., L&GBM, PhD Thesis, School of Engineering, UFRGS, Porto Alegre, Brazil, 2013.

stability of the production process, which reduced the OTIF from 99% to 80%, meant that resources were focused on getting the stability and customer satisfaction back to acceptable levels. At the third site there was a high level of employee engagement and also desire to improve. However, although there was stability, the level of deployment had not yet progressed to value stream level and production cells did not exist. This made the task of prioritizing the benefits of the L&GBM against the more significant benefits of achieving flow quite a challenge as the benefits of flow production were far greater than could be achieved through the L&GBM Kaizen. Following those, it is possible to highlight and conclude the following topics related to the application of the L&GBM for a cell in different business environments:

- *Regarding the confirmation of whether the five-step model proposed and structure for the L&GBM for a cell can be applied to any type of manufacturing business*: Although the application did not succeed completely in any of the three cases, this was not due to the characteristics of the model itself, which was generic to all the sites in which it was presented, but due to restrictions of the three businesses in accomplishing the model prerequisites.

- *Confirming the prerequisites, considering different manufacturing environments:* The prerequisites were confirmed. All the requirements that were not achieved by the sites became barriers to the model deployment.
- *Analyzing potential savings in terms of environmental improvements and cost reduction after applying the model:* The two Kaizens conducted presented ideas that would represent significant reduction of cost and improvement in the use of mass and energy flows.
- *Reviewing ways of working when applying the model in different business conditions:* The model itself is straightforward and simple to be implemented. One key thing to be taken into consideration when applying the model to other businesses is to make sure that the seven prerequisites are fully implemented.

Therefore, considering these results and the difficulties in implementing the L&GBM in different manufacturing environments, the conclusion is that the implementation of the following seven prerequisites are key to its success and application of the model.

A more detailed discussion about the model will be presented in Chapter 3.

L&GBM WAYS TO SAVE MASS AND ENERGY

As discussed previously, the objective of environmental thinking can be described in one dimension, with two main focuses:

- Reduce the use of natural resources to maximize productivity
- Minimum environmental impact

Environmental practices such as (1) cleaner production, (2) ecoefficiency, and (3) life-cycle analysis (LCA) are focused in reducing the use of resources, improving productivity, as well as reducing environmental impact.

The concept of the L&GBM is linking Lean thinking with environmental problems, by adding one more aspect to traditional Lean thinking: the environment. In this context, the main objectives of the model are based on the fundamental building blocks of all other environmental sustainable practices (such as cleaner production, ecoefficiency, and life-cycle analysis), which are,

- Improving the productivity of manufacturing processes resources by optimizing the environmental performance, through the optimization of the use of resources (materials and energy consumption and wastes generation)
- Reducing the impact of manufacturing processes on the environment, by reducing all the environmental wastes generated by production

As the other environmental practices, L&GBM intends to minimize waste and emissions and to maximize productive output. Considering the model fundamental building blocks and the Lean principles, this section highlights some of the practical improvement ideas that were identified during the Kaizens events, for both first and second levels of flow. These ideas are reviewed against the L&GBM and Lean principles and are presented in the Table 2.20.

In order to understand these ideas, Table 2.21 highlights examples for the improvement opportunities identified during the Kaizens.

These are just some of the examples identified during the Kaizen events. The ideas presented here do not substitute the learning and sharing of experiences created during the Kaizen events by the involved teams but do give a flavor of what can be produced by the teams.

TABLE 2.20

Ten L&GBM Ways to Save Mass and Energy

Improvement Opportunity	Application Level	Alignment to L&GBM Principles: (1) Efficiency in the Use of Natural Resources (2) Reduction of Environmental Impact	Alignment to Lean Principles
Turn things off that are not being used	Level 1 flow	Yes—use of resources efficiently Less power = less generation = less CO_2	Yes—overprocessing and waste of energy
Turn things off that are waiting to be used	Level 1 flow	Yes—use of resources efficiently Less power = less generation = less CO_2	Yes—overprocessing and waste of energy
Redesign the product and process to be closer to the final specification and easier to make	Level 1 and 2 flow	Yes—Green design/ design for Green manufacturing, less waste produced, less resources (both material and energy)	Yes—consider process efficiency as well as product manufacturing efficiency
Stop doing things	Level 1 flow	Yes—eliminate the use of resources, less resources used	Yes—fundamental primary challenge of achieving customer value
Use different products that have less of an environmental impact	Level 1 and 2 flow	Yes, but must consider whole life cycle environmental impact	Yes—alignment to customer value through functional needs assessment
Ensure standards are in place and used	Level 1 flow	Marginal—standardizing this eliminates waste caused by variation	Yes—use of standard work, job instruction—"make it flow"
Use energy/ materials from one process to support another	Level 2 flow	Yes—maximize the use of resources in manufacturing by reusing the original energy to perform another activity	Yes—less waste of energy/materials through reuse
Use cold instead of hot	Level 1 and 2 flow	Yes—by reducing the demand for heat energy	Yes—less waste of energy
Challenge paradigms	Level 1 and 2 flow	Yes—eventually	Yes—continuous improvement

Source: Developed by the authors.

TABLE 2.21

Examples of 10 L&GBM Ways to Save Mass and Energy

Improvement Opportunity	Examples	Comments
Turn things off that are not being used	Turn things off that are not being used, for example, 1. Lights 2. Power 3. Air 4. Water 5. Motors	It may sound simple to turn off things that are not being used but quite often there is laziness in the factory to consider these things. In one pilot Kaizens all the machines were left running when there was no product to machine. The staff and managers were left bemused at their own ignorance of the situation when it was pointed out to them. Sometimes the obvious is not seen if it is there every day.
Turn things off that are waiting to be used	Turn things off that are waiting to be used, such as 1. Standby machines 2. Conveyors 3. Vehicle engines 4. Motors 5. Lights 6. Power 7. Air	Similar to the previous one, the L&GBM Kaizen prompted the thinking to challenge the status quo.
Redesign the product and process to be closer to the final specification and easier to make	Re-design the product to be closer to the final specification, for example, 1. Less waste produced—chips 2. Less offcuts	A more difficult challenge as this will invariably involve discussions with several key stakeholders and the customer. However for mass production items, small changes can make significant savings over the life time of the product. *(Continued)*

TABLE 2.21 (*Continued*)

Examples of 10 L&GBM Ways to Save Mass and Energy

Improvement Opportunity	Examples	Comments
Stop doing things	Stop doing things, such as wet lubrication replaced with dry cooling	A fundamental challenge to see if historic practices can be ceased or if technology can help to solve the problem in a different way.
Use different products that have less of an environmental impact	Use different products that have less of an environmental impact 1. Water-based lubricants vs. oil-based lubricant 2. Paper instead of plastic 3. Reuse or recycle	Consideration needs to be given to using alternative products or methods to achieve the same goal. In one of the Kaizens ran the introduction of reusable pallets instead of one-way plastic packaging.
Ensure standards are in place	Ensure standards are in place, used, and continually improved: 1. For chemical concentrations 2. For mixes 3. For production processes	Over time, standards should evolve to encompass good practice; however, quite often standards erode or opportunities for improvement fail to be identified.
Use energy/materials from one process to support another	Use energy from one process to support another: 1. Heat exchangers 2. Kinetic recovery 3. Brake regeneration	As environmental awareness grows more and more ways are developed to reuse energy in its different forms.
Use cold instead of hot	Use cold instead of hot for 1. Cleaning 2. Washing	As the aforementioned practices, this challenges the existing standards to see if they can be achieved in a less impactful way. Just placing them under review brings the opportunity to the fore.

(*Continued*)

TABLE 2.21 (*Continued*)

Examples of 10 L&GBM Ways to Save Mass and Energy

Improvement Opportunity	Examples	Comments
Challenge paradigms	Be more efficient—use less 1. Replace standard lights with low energy 2. Insulate—use less heat/less cold 3. Turn down thermostats, water temperatures, oil temperatures, and mixing temperatures 4. Established processes and standards 5. Experiment to see if less environmental inputs can achieve the same standards	These obvious targets should be the low-hanging fruit that is surfaced at the early stages of the Kaizen. More challenging is to get to the heart of the production process to see what can be reduced without impacting. Bringing Lean thinkers to the Kaizen should enable more radical ideas for change.

Source: Developed by the authors.

3

Lean and Green Business Model Strategic Implementation

KEY LESSONS FROM IMPLEMENTATION

Table 3.1 presents the conclusions and results achieved through the application of the L&GBM related to

1. Reduction of environmental impact and the subsequent productivity increase in the use of resources
2. The percentage of the action plan that was implemented
3. The percentage of cost reduction that was achieved
4. The total direct cost savings made
5. The confirmation of prerequisites required to make it work

The data used for developing these conclusions are based on the results presented in Chapter 2.

Based on Table 3.1, the following can be concluded:

- For the cells that accomplished all the model prerequisites, the reduction of environmental impact and productivity increase through the better use of resources, and the application of the L&GBM for a cell is able to reduce the use of resources by an average of 35%. For the sister cells, the model is able to reduce the use of resources by 20%. L&GBM for VS, comparing 2011 with 2012 environmental performance, confirmed VS improvement in terms of reduction of environmental impact and increase in the productivity in the use of resources by 12%.
- In terms of cost reduction, with the implementation of actions averaging 65% of the improvement plans, the results show a potential

TABLE 3.1

L&GBM Improvement Cycles Analysis

L&GBM Analysis	Results in Terms of (1) Reduction of Environmental Impact; (2) Increase the Productivity in the Use of Resources[a]	% of Action Plan Implementation	% Cost Reduction in Mass and Energy	Total Direct L&GBM Cost Savings	Confirmation of the Seven Prerequisites
Improvement cycle 1					
Analysis of the application and results of the L&GBM for a cell pilot testing	Cell 1: 50% Cell 2: 40%	Cell 1: 94% Cell 2: 81%	Cell 1: 13% Cell 2: 3%	US$ 147,000	Yes
Improvement cycle 2					
Analysis of the application and results of the L&GBM for a cell roll out	Cell 3: 50% Cell 4: 40% Cell 5: 27% Cell 6: 17% Cell 7: 31% Cell 8: 34% Cell 9: 34%	Cell 3: 68% Cell 4: 86% Cell 5: 40% Cell 6: 55% Cell 7: 60% Cell 8: 58% Cell 9: 50%	Cell 3: 6,3% Cell 4: 19% Cell 5: 4% Cell 6: 11% Cell 7: 4% Cell 8: 2% Cell 9: 8%	US$ 419,645	Yes
Improvement cycle 3					
Analysis of the application and results of the L&GBM for sister cells	4.1–4.2: 31% 9.1–9.4: 15% 9.5–9.8: 15%	4.1–4.2: 65% 9.1–9.4: 14% 9.5–9.8: 18%	4.1–4.2: 3.5% 9.1–9.4: 0.5% 9.5–9.8: 1%	R$ 28,844	Yes

(Continued)

TABLE 3.1 (*Continued*)

L&GBM Improvement Cycles Analysis

L&GBM Analysis	Results in Terms of (1) Reduction of Environmental Impact; (2) Increase the Productivity in the Use of Resources[a]	% of Action Plan Implementation	% Cost Reduction in Mass and Energy	Total Direct L&GBM Cost Savings	Confirmation of the Seven Prerequisites
Improvement cycle 4					
Analysis of the application and results of the L&GBM for a value stream	Energy: 7% Metallic wastes: 6% Water: 2% Oils: 6% Contaminated wastes: 40%	21%	Energy: +6.1% (increase in tariffs) Metallic wastes: 7.3% Water: 11% Oils: 0.1% Contaminated wastes: 32% Overall mass and energy reduction (2011 × 2012): 4.5%	US$ 795,439	Yes
Improvement cycle 5					
Analysis of the application and results of the L&GBM for a cell in different manufacturing environments	Aerospace—6% Automotive—7% Metals—Kaizen was not developed	Aerospace—0% Automotive—not informed Metals—Kaizen was not developed	Aerospace—0% Automotive—not informed Metals—Kaizen was not developed	Not possible to calculate	Yes

Source: Pampanelli, A., L&GBM, PhD Thesis, School of Engineering, UFRGS, Porto Alegre, Brazil, 2013.

[a] For cell level = Kaizen results/For VS level = Measured results.

of reducing by 8% the total cost with mass and energy flows after applying the L&GBM for a cell. For sister cells this result is limited to only 2% of potential cost reduction. For the value stream level, a 21% implementation of the action plan, generated direct cost savings of US$795,439.00 and an overall mass and energy reduction (2011 × 2012) of 4.5%. In terms of direct cost savings, these four L&GBM improvement cycles produced alone a total of US$ 1.39 m in savings.

- In terms of confirmation of model prerequisites, the pilot testing, the roll out of the model for a cell, and the application of the model for a cell in other manufacturing businesses confirm the L&GBM for cell prerequisites. The cells that accomplished the seven prerequisites achieved better results. The Kaizens developed outside of Brazil that failed did not have (1) the right leadership support in place, (2) a high level of Lean deployment, and (3) a structure for data collection.

For L&GBM, the data tells us the story that prework preparation and data collection are the key steps and should be developed comprehensively in order to get good results during the Kaizen event. Most of the events developed outside of Brazil had a lack of resources and structure for developing steps 3 and 4 of the L&GBM for a cell. Therefore, a new prerequisite related to data collection was introduced to improve the model. The L&GBM prerequisites were also confirmed for the model for sister cell and for the value stream level.

Table 3.2 presents the identification of key findings, model improvement opportunities, as well as the changes developed along the research in order to incorporate the improvement opportunities into the original model for all five improvement cycles.

Therefore, following what was presented in Tables 3.1 and 3.2, the following conclusions can be made so far about the L&GBM application and results:

- *Findings that confirm L&GBM objectives of (1) reduction of environmental impact and (2) increasing the productivity in the use of resources.* As presented in Table 3.1, in terms of a reduction of environmental impact and increasing the productivity in the use of resources, for the first and second levels of flow that accomplished all the model prerequisites, the application of the L&GBM for a cell is able to reduce, on average, 35% of the use of resources.

TABLE 3.2

Improvement Cycles Key Finding and Improvement Opportunities

	Key Findings and Observations	Improvement Opportunities	Actions Taken
Improvement cycle 1 Analysis of the L&GBM for a cell pilot testing	1. *Confirming all the prerequisites: The cell is a good starting point for a Lean and Green intervention*—where the things are happening and where people can "touch" the flow of production and can easily see the supporting flows (mass and energy) 2. *Lean stability, deployment level is a good starting point* 3. *Management support is key:* For developing the Kaizen, for the action plan implementation, and to show business intent for the initiative 4. *Kaizen approach is successful for environmental improvement:* Bottom-up team effort; use of employee involvement raised the environmental understanding to a much higher level 5. *Lean and Green is an excellent pollution prevention strategy:* Capable of reducing energy by 10% and materials and wastes by 50%	1. *Involvement of key specialists:* Need for accounting involvement—to validate the financial results; need for specific expertise for running the Kaizen—facilities, environment, and maintenance; engineering should also be part of the Kaizen teams in order to support the development and deployment of ideas 2. *Implementation of action plans follow-up strategy:* Need to set responsibilities and deadlines within the team before the Kaizen is finished in order to have a better deployment of the action plan implementation process; need to keep communication process alive after Kaizen is ended 3. *Strategy for sister cells:* Need to establish a strategy for spreading results to other similar cells without losing the environmental learning of the Kaizen	1. *Definition of a list of key specialists to be involved during the Kaizens* (accounting, facilities, environment, maintenance, and engineering) 2. *Definition of a strategy for action plan follow-up* 3. *Creation of the L&GBM for sisters cells* All these ideas were already implemented and tested in the application of the Lean and Green model: (1) roll out, (2) sisters' cells, and (3) testing of the model in different manufacturing environments (Continued)

TABLE 3.2 (*Continued*)

Improvement Cycles Key Finding and Improvement Opportunities

	Key Findings and Observations	Improvement Opportunities	Actions Taken
Improvement cycle 2	1. *Confirming all the prerequisites—Lean stability and deployment level is key for Lean and Green: Kaizens should not be developed in cells that do not have a deployment level of Lean*	1. *Definition of Lean and Green expectations—system design:* Need to define system design/expectations for Lean and Green—	1. *The objective for L&GBM for a cell were set.* This idea was implemented; better results were confirmed along 2012
Analysis of L&GBM model for a cell roll out	Development of Kaizens in cells that did not have a good level of Lean deployment proved that this needed to be in place in order to start Lean and Green	1. Output 2. Pathway 3. Connections 4. SW	
	2. *For first level flow model is more dependent on Lean (change agents) than environmental expertise; improvement actions are simpler*		
Improvement cycle 3	1. *Confirming all the prerequisites of the model*	1. *None*	1. *Leadership should be aware that a less complicated Kaizen may not produce the same cost and environmental results.* This model was not applied in any other cell along 2012
Analysis of L&GBM model for sisters' cells	2. *A shorter Kaizen delivers worse results—* although it keeps the employee involvement, the idea of developing a less complicated Kaizen, with less involvement of experts and less application of resources does not maintain the same level of cost and environmental improvement achieved by the L&GBM for a cell		

(*Continued*)

TABLE 3.2 (*Continued*)

Improvement Cycles Key Finding and Improvement Opportunities

	Key Findings and Observations	Improvement Opportunities	Actions Taken
	1. *Confirming the prerequisites specially related to environmental focus and concern:* L&GBM for a value stream environmental focus is higher; L&GBM for a value stream requires a higher level of environmental understanding and competence in order to develop the analysis, the Kaizen, and set the action plan; therefore, environmental language needs to be translated to manufacturing; understanding about the key factors is key here		
Improvement cycle 4 Analysis of L&GBM for a value stream	2. *At the value stream level, the data tells the story* 3. *For the value stream analysis, for an environmental perspective, it should be a site-based environmental impact and not only the impact of one value stream;* there is a combination of environmental effects that can create a system interference changing the overall impact; therefore, traditional VSM thinking (divided by product families) is not applicable because it will not consider the overall impact on the surroundings and the combination of environmental effects	1. *Shop floor environmental review strategy for a value stream:* Need to create a standard for value stream L&GBM analysis in order to translate environmental language to manufacturing terms	1. *A strategy for shop floor environmental review for L&GBM for a value stream;* This idea was already implemented in 2012

(Continued)

TABLE 3.2 (Continued)

Improvement Cycles Key Finding and Improvement Opportunities

	Key Findings and Observations	Improvement Opportunities	Actions Taken
Improvement cycle 5 Analysis of the L&GBM for a cell in different manufacturing environments	1. *Confirming all the prerequisites:* a. Lean deployment level is critical b. Operational stability is a core requirement c. Leadership support is critical along all eight steps of model development d. Top-down and bottom-up required for success 2. *Lean and Green should be the continuation of a continuous improvement culture:* Should not be seen as a new initiative—should be integrated to the Lean structure in place 3. *The involvement of specialists:* Finance and other core function support are key	1. *Lack of data collection structure:* For Lean and Green the data tells us the story, so prework preparation and data collection are key steps and should be developed properly in other to get good results during the Kaizen event; Most of the events developed outside Brazil failed due to lack of support, resources, and structure for developing steps 3 and 4 of the L&GBM for a cell.	1. *A new prerequisite related to data collection should be introduced in the L&GBM* This idea was implemented and tested along 2012. The model presented in Chapter 2 considers this new prerequisite.

Source: Pampanelli, A., L&GBM, PhD Thesis, School of Engineering, UFRGS, Porto Alegre, Brazil, 2013.

For the sister cell case, the model is able to reduce 20%. In the value stream level, the model is able to reduce 12% of the use of resources.

- *Findings that confirm L&GBM potential for cost savings*: As presented in Table 3.1, in terms of cost reduction, the results show a potential of reducing by 2%–8% of the total cost with mass and energy flows (8% for cells, 2% for sister cell, and 4.5% for the value stream level). In terms of direct cost savings, these four L&GBM improvement cycles produced a total of US$1.39 m of savings. Cagno et al. (2005) analyzed cleaner production and profitability based on the results from 134 industrial pollution prevention projects. For the automotive sector, which includes companies such as Chrysler, Ford, and General Motors, the average annual savings obtained was US$318500/year. This represents only 20% of what may be possible under the L&GBM. Also, traditional Lean thinking considers only reduction of the seven classic wastes. With the introduction of the environmental variable concern along the flow of value, L&GBM proves that other sources of wastes may be focused and reduced, thus maximizing the overall savings. As already mentioned in Chapter 2 the original logic does not take into consideration the other sources of cost that are part of the manufacturing process, the environmental wastes (materials and energy consumption and wastes generation), and that are not considered in the original Rich's model. Therefore, the L&GBM is builds on Rich's model by adding one extra variable to it to be capable of promoting manufacturing excellence and cost reduction, the environmental variable.

- *Findings that confirm the prerequisites*: A number of variables must be considered when applying the model. The pilot testing, the roll out of the model, and the application to other businesses outside of Brazil confirmed the prerequisites. The following attributes should be in place to apply the L&GBM:
  1. A stable process, with delivery records over 90%
  2. A sufficient deployment level in terms of using and applying Lean tools
  3. EI (employee involvement) systems in place
  4. A supportive management team
  5. Environmental awareness among the members
  6. Significant use of natural resources
  7. Data collection structure

The cells that fulfilled all prerequisites, including achieving a deployment level of Lean in terms of applying Lean tools and a stable process, achieved better results.

- *Improvement opportunities that proposed changes in the prerequisites*: As presented in Table 3.2, following the results of the application of the L&GBM for a cell in different manufacturing environments, a new prerequisite related to data collection was introduced in the L&GBM in order to cope with what was found after the testing process.
- *Improvement opportunities that proposed general changes in the model and Kaizen structure and application*: As presented in Table 3.2, general improvement opportunities were identified after each improvement cycle developed.

After a full evaluation of these results, it is possible to confirm that the L&GBM is a good and practical example of how Lean "ways of working," based on the Kaizen spirit of involving people, can support sustainable manufacturing.

POSITIONING THE L&GBM

What comes after sustainability?

Compression thinking (Hall, 2010) may answer this question.

With a top-level statement that establishes "Assure survival of life and promote quality of life using processes that work to perfection with self-correcting, self-learning systems. No use of excess resources. No wasted energy. No toxic releases. Quality over quantity, always." Compression thinking is based on the fact that the society is near a turning point; the end of expansion. Population is expanding on an earth with finite resources. Old thinking from the industrial revolution and financial thinking need to be changed. So, the case for compression is based on four main drivers:

1. Finite resources
2. Precarious environment
3. Overconsumption
4. Pushback—as shown in Figure 3.1

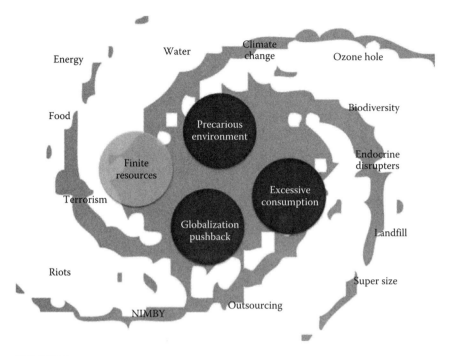

FIGURE 3.1
The case for compression. (From Hall, R., *Compression: Meeting the Challenges of Sustainability through Vigorous Learning Enterprises*, CRC Press, Boca Raton, FL, 2010.)

According to Hall (2010), Lean thinking breaks a little from that, since Lean practitioners are used to removing waste from processes, not always represented by costs. However, compression thinking goes beyond just removing waste from a system. Physical actions and their consequences must take priority over financial motivations. Conceptual basics that are part of compression thinking are well-known, but practice is slow to take hold. First, eliminate waste—things that add no value to anyone. Then conserve (reuse, repair, remanufacture, recycle, and so on) and contain (hazardous material). Many individuals want to decrease their resource footprints, but until organizations create practical systems they can use, their effect is minimal. Therefore, compression begs for a fundamentally new economic thinking, looking behind financial transactions to see the physical reality of what society and corporations do. Also, compression is not purely environmental. Environmental concerns are only one reason to make systemic changes. It calls for a different mind-set, for an integrated approach in order to deal with the increasing complexity of today's work.

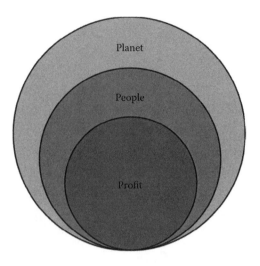

FIGURE 3.2
The three vectors presented by the sustainability concept based on compression thinking. (From Hall, R., Compression thinking, in *LERC Annual Conference 2011, Proceedings*, 10th edn, Cardiff University, Cardiff, U.K., 2011, pp. 13–28.)

Figure 3.2 shows how the three vectors presented by the sustainability concept are viewed based on compression thinking.

Following this, compression thinking proposes a new way to see environmental issues. Differently than the sustainability concept, it states that this should be part of bigger system, integrated into the core business model. Although compression has a much wider scope, it is understood that Lean thinking may be a way to get into compression. Understanding the roles of sustainability and compression concepts is fundamental for the development of this work.

Figure 3.3 presents the position of L&GBM comparing it to pure Lean and pure Green thinking and how it integrates the sustainability vectors in order to drive compression that fundamentally begs for equity and for a new economic thinking.

The L&GBM is a model that intends to motivate a conceptual transition, in a learning process that integrates different pieces of knowledge.

Prior concepts, such as pure Lean and Green thinking, are the baggage.

While integrating such concepts, L&GBM proposes to create a new model where it brings in the following:

1. Productivity in the use of natural resources
2. Impact reduction

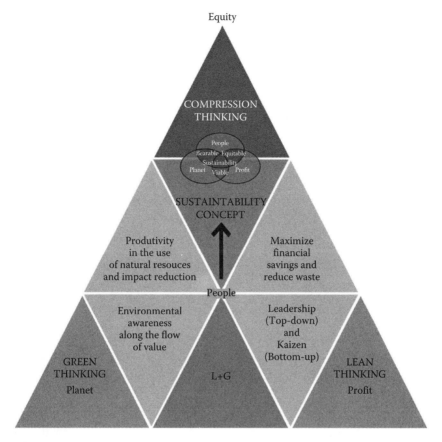

FIGURE 3.3
Positioning the L&GBM. (From Pampanelli, A., L&GBM, PhD Thesis, School of Engineering, UFRGS, Porto Alegre, Brazil, 2013.)

3. Environmental awareness
4. Financial savings
5. People involvement
6. Leadership

All the above are originally derived from different sources, and are now connected as fundamental blocks of a new way of thinking.

As time passes, L&GBM seeks not only the integration of the social, environmental, and financial, but also equity, equitable value, importance, and priority for all its vectors, promoting connectedness within and outside the system.

CONFIRMING L&GBM KEY CHARACTERISTICS: IDENTIFYING PRECONDITIONS FOR SUCCESS

Following the real life results and the model presented in Part II, the differences between pure Green thinking, pure Lean thinking, and the L&GBM are summarized as follows:

- *The L&GBM fully integrates Lean thinking and Green thinking*, merging the fundamental principles of Lean (i.e., the five key principles; Womack and Jones, 1996) and Green (1) improving the use of natural resources and (2) reducing environmental impact (Moreira et al., 2010) philosophies to create a unique, integrated model.
- *The L&GBM introduces a new dimension into traditional Lean thinking—environmental concerns.* Traditional Lean thinking focuses on four dimensions: safety, quality, delivery, and cost (Bicheno, 2000). The L&GBM introduces environmental concerns by requiring (1) the productive use of resources, (2) a reduction in environmental impact, and (3) environmental awareness along the flow of value.
- *The L&GBM is a model that proposes a conceptual transition:* L&GBM proposes to create a new model where it brings in (1) Productivity in the use of natural resources, (2) Impact reduction, (3) Environmental awareness, (4) Financial savings, (5) People involvement and (6) Leadership.

These are originally derived from different sources and are now connected as fundamental blocks of a new way of thinking. As time passes, L&GBM seeks not only the integration of the social, environmental and financial, but also equity, equitable value, importance, and priority for all its vectors, promoting connectedness within and outside the system.

- *L&GBM has its own purpose*: "Producing exactly what the customer wants, exactly when (with no delay), at fair price and minimum waste and environmental impact and the maximum productivity in the use of natural resources."

- *L&GBM has its own principles*:
  1. Identify a stable value stream (level 1, 2, or 3)
  2. Identify in the flow of value the environmental aspects and impacts
  3. Measure VS environmental impacts and the use of natural resources
  4. Identify alternatives to
     (1) impact reduction and (2) resources productivity in VS
  5. Pursue perfection—continuous improvement
- *L&GBM has its own ways of working*: L&GBM will be integrated as part of the continuous improvement process of a manufacturing process, where the Lean philosophy and ways of working are already in place. Following this, the substance of the study of the L&GBM are the mass–energy flows of the manufacturing processes. The expected output for model application is the achievement of improvements in these flows (materials, chemicals, water, waste, effluent, and energy), contributing to improvement of the overall performance.
- *The L&GBM focuses on nontraditional sources of savings*: Traditional Lean thinking considers only reductions in the seven classic Lean wastes. With the introduction of environmental concerns along the flow of value, other sources of waste identified while analyzing the supporting flows of production (energy, materials, water, etc.) can be targeted and reduced, thereby maximizing overall savings. This idea supports the study of Moreira et al. (2010) and Brown et al. (2014), which explores other sources of waste, environmental impacts, energy use, materials consumption, and emissions to show that environmental waste is hidden within the seven classic production wastes (Ohno, 1988).
- *The L&GB prioritizes manufacturing stability and a focus on the customer*: The first step involves delivering what the customer wants, specifying the customer value, and then identifying the value streams, thereby making value flow at the pull of the customer. The L&GBM's name suggests that it is necessary to be Lean *first*. Therefore, a sufficient Lean deployment level is key to implementing the L&GBM. This idea supports the study of Dues et al. (2012), which concluded that a Lean environment serves as a catalyst to facilitate environmental sustainability.
- *L&GBM thus requires a certain level of manufacturing stability and Lean deployment prior to being introduced*: Other environmental practices,

such as cleaner production (Cagno et al., 2005) and ecoefficiency (Korhone, 2007) do not take these prerequisites into consideration.

- As with other environmental practices, the L&GBM has the clear objective of improving the use of natural resources and reducing the environmental impact (Moreira et al., 2010). In this case, the difference between the L&GBM and other environmental practices is the approach that the L&GBM adopts to implement environmental practices. Both cleaner production and ecoefficiency focus on analyzing the flow of materials and energy in a company to identify improvement opportunities, such as the use of fewer resources; the minimization of waste, emissions, and pollution; and the maximization of product output. Neither cleaner production nor ecoefficiency focuses on manufacturing approaches to manufacturing and value streams (Womack and Jones, 1996) to accomplish this objective. The L&GBM identifies and measures environmental aspects and impacts as well as inputs and outputs, based on manufacturing value streams and respecting the real flow of value. Applying the L&GBM makes it easier to coordinate environmental and production performance metrics in a unique and integrated system.

- *The L&GBM focuses on a simultaneous top-down and bottom-up approach for deploying continuous environmental improvements*: All improvement opportunities that are identified by the L&GBM model using the Kaizen approach (Berger, 1997) are directly integrated into continuous improvement of the already existing structure due to Lean deployment.

After a full evaluation of these findings, it is possible to demonstrate that the L&GBM is different from Green thinking, pure Lean thinking, and other existing approaches, that is a model that fully integrates Lean thinking and Green thinking, merging the fundamental principles, introducing a new dimension into traditional Lean thinking, and motivating conceptual transition between both concepts in a way to achieve sustainability.

---

20 QUESTIONS AND 20 ANSWERS FOR THE L&GBM

Part II presented the L&GBM. In order to put together all the ideas that created L&GBM, the model was successively reviewed in reflective process of problem solving, with the support of global business and academic

TABLE 3.3

L&GBM Response to Specialist's Inputs

Source of the Input	Main Questions	How L&GBM Is Addressing It?
Global environmental specialists	1. Need for management support	Leadership support is the fourth prerequisite for implementing L&GBM
Global environmental specialists	2. Need for resources	A structure in place for data collection is the seventh for implementing L&GBM Lean and Green is data dependent: As in many environmental sustainable practices, such as cleaner production, for L&GBM the data tells us the story, so prework preparation and data collection are key steps and should be developed properly in order to get good results during the Kaizen event
Global environmental specialists	3. Need for implementers and experts	For first level flow, L&GBM for a cell is more dependent on Lean (change agents) than environmental expertise: Improvement actions are simpler. So, for this case, the already existing Lean structure can support this gap. L&GBM for a value stream requires a higher level of environmental understanding and competence in order to develop the analysis, the Kaizen, and set the action plan. So, in this case, it the support of experts will be necessary
Global environmental specialists	4. Need to be prioritized	L&GBM has a Lean to Green approach: the application should be the continuation; a second step of a continuous improvement/Lean culture already in place. So, from a business perspective, it only should be prioritized if the company already reached a certain level in its Lean (continuous improvement) journey and is able to accomplish all model prerequisites
Global environmental specialists	5. Technology access	The L&GBM for a cell does not involve major changes in technology. Rather, the model focuses on behavioral and operations efficiency changes (several examples are presented in Chapter 2). Technology access should be analyzed when expanding the model for second or third level of flow, as shown in Section 6.4. The projects that are implemented in the VS level require a higher level of technology and expertise and it may be a barrier depending where the model is implemented.

(Continued)

TABLE 3.3 (Continued)

L&GBM Response to Specialist's Inputs

Source of the Input	Main Questions	How L&GBM Is Addressing It?
Global environmental specialists	6. Need to deal with worldwide differences	Since the global application of the L&GBM was limited this question could not be answered totally and this is a limitation for this study.
Academia	7. Is a Lean to Green approach better than just going Green?	The answer based on the results achieved from all of the tests for this case is positive. In the model it can be translated in the two first prerequisites presented: (1) The cell had a deployment level in applying Lean tools and (2) a stable process. The results presented showed that the cells that had a deployment level in applying and using Lean tools not only achieved better results for improving its mass and energy flows but also were able to implement the action plans faster. In the pilot testing, Cell 1 and Cell 2 proposed an average reduction of materials and energy usage from 40% to 50% after applying the L&GBM. If we consider the case of Cell 2, although the cost reduction figures were not very high, the work in a Kaizen approach proposed actions that were able to reduce the usage of cleaning cloths by 50% and the wasted grease by 100%. It represents that Lean to Green is better than just going Green. All this means that using an existing manufacturing improvement culture can be an excellent pollution prevention strategy. Respecting the manufacturing ways of working and mind-set represented here by the Lean thinking culture and using it in favor of the environment can be a good strategy for consolidating sustainability concept in the shop floor, where profit, people, and planet issues are equally balanced.
Academia	8. And better than just going Lean?	The answer to this question is also positive. Applying L&GBM, it was possible not only to improve environmental performance (from 12% to 35% in average) but also to identify and eliminate other sources of wastes that traditional Lean thinking does not focus. This extra source of cost reduction represents 2%–8% reduction of the total cost of mass and energy flows of a manufacturing process.

(Continued)

TABLE 3.3 (Continued)

L&GBM Response to Specialist's Inputs

Source of the Input	Main Questions	How L&GBM Is Addressing It?
Academia	9. And better than just going Green?	The answer to this question is positive too. Most environmental practices focus on the same objects of study: improving mass and energy flows performance and reducing impact. The difference, if compared pure Green practices with L&GBM, is not what to do but how you do it. Kiperstok (2000) once said: "If cleaner production practices so obviously make a common sense, why do they not occur naturally in industry?"
		Traditional Green practice fight for the same resources, time, and space than manufacturing. They want to be prioritized, replacing other continuous improvement initiatives. L&GBM not only explain why to do it, but also creates a space to really do it, merging it in the original manufacturing improvement culture.
		The result of L&GBM proves to be more effective. Comparing L&GBM results with the studies of Cagno et al. (2005), L&GBM is four times more effective in terms of cost savings than Green practices.
Academia	10. What are the real differences between pure Lean, pure Green, and the L&GBM?	As already discussed in Chapter 2
		1. L&GBM prioritizes the customer focus
		2. L&GBM identifies and measures environmental aspects and impacts based on value streams
		3. L&GBM focuses on a top-down and bottom-up approach
		4. L&GBM prioritizes maximizing value and reducing costs
		5. L&GBM introduces into the traditional Lean thinking a new dimension—the environmental concern aspect
		6. L&GBM focus on other sources of savings

(Continued)

TABLE 3.3 (Continued)

L&GBM Response to Specialist's Inputs

Source of the Input	Main Questions	How L&GBM Is Addressing It?
Academia	11. What are L&GBM prerequisites?	1. A stable process, with delivery records over 90%
		2. A mature deployment level in using and applying Lean tools
		3. Employee involvement (EI) systems are in place
		4. A supportive management team
		5. Good level of environmental awareness
		6. Significant use of natural resources
		7. Structure in place for environmental data collection
Academia	12. What are the L&GBM dimensions?	L&GBM has five dimensions: safety, quality, delivery, cost, and environment. L&GBM is built based on Rich's model, adding one extra variable to it: process stability (safety + quality + delivery + flexibility) + environment → cost reduction
Academia	13. What is the main purpose of L&GBM?	The general purpose model can be described as "Producing exactly what the customer wants, exactly when (with no delay), at a fair price and with minimum waste and environmental impact by delivering the maximum productivity in the use of natural resources." It means that the Lean and Green thinking will be described in five dimensions: (1) safety, (2) quality, (3) delivery, (4) cost, and (5) environment. The L&GBM is a model that intends to motivate to a conceptual transition, in a learning process that integrates different pieces of knowledge

(*Continued*)

TABLE 3.3 (*Continued*)

L&GBM Response to Specialist's Inputs

Source of the Input	Main Questions	How L&GBM Is Addressing It?
Academia	14. What is the level of leadership that L&GBM requires? Is it necessary to have in place the right leadership support and employee involvement tools along with others to achieve good results with a L&GBM?	A supportive management team. Leadership support is the fourth prerequisite for implementing L&GBM. L&GBM requires a top-down and bottom-up approach, so it needs the right level of leadership and people involvement in order to succeed. In the model it was translated in the third and fourth prerequisites: (1) The cell already had EI Systems in place and (2) It had good management support for developing and implementing the Kaizen initiatives. This is the case for the application of the L&GBM outside GKN Brazil. In average, all cells in GKN Brazil were able to implement the improvement opportunities identified during the Kaizen. They had the support from their leaders for developing the changes and the right EI tools in place for tracking the implementation. It means that the same behavioral and involvement attitude that is part of the Lean Kaizens is also applicable and valid for an environmental Kaizen as well. The Kaizens developed outside GKN Brazil failed also due to lack of leadership support in place
Academia	15. In order to achieve good results is it necessary to be a cell with intensive use of material and energy?	The answer to this is negative. In the model this was attributed to the final prerequisite that the cell needed to have a significant use of resources and waste generation in order to be a case for L&GBM intervention. Cell 2 did not present this characteristic. It is an assembly cell, where 75% of its resources usage is the grease that is applicable inside the final product. Although, in terms of cost savings, it did not present such impressive results, in terms of pollution prevention the improvement ideas proposed by the employees represented an average of 40% of mass and energy cell consumption. Considering that the main objective for developing a cell environmental Kaizen is improving its supporting flows performance (materials and energy consumption and wastes generation) this result can be achieved even in cells where the use of materials is not so intensive. This is also the case for Cell 4 and Cell 9. They do not have so intense a use of resources but are presenting good results also in reducing mass and energy flows

(*Continued*)

TABLE 3.3 (Continued)

L&GBM Response to Specialist's Inputs

Source of the Input	Main Questions	How L&GBM Is Addressing It?
Academia	16. The level of environmental improvement depends of a preexisting condition. How is this topic taken in consideration in the model?	For applying L&GBM it is required for a cell to have a good level of environmental awareness and for the second level flow that factory is ISO 14001 certified and it is in its second improvement cycle. So, minimum level of environmental concern and improvement is required prior to implementation. That is the cut line for implementing the model
Academia	17. Why most of the L&GBM application outside GKN Brazil failed?	The first reason is related to the accomplishment of L&GBM prerequisites: The Kaizens that failed did not have the right leadership support in place and a good level of Lean deployment. A second reason was also identified: lack of data collection structure. This is a strong premise for any environmental practice and also L&GBM. For L&GBM, the data tells us the story, so prework preparation and data collection are key steps and should be developed properly in other to get good results during the Kaizen event. Most of the events developed outside Brazil had a lack of resources and structure for developing Steps 3 and 4 of the Lean and Green model for a cell. Therefore, a new prerequisite related to data collection should be introduced in the Lean and Green model
Academia	18. Since L&GBM outside Brazil failed, is it context specific?	The L&GBM is a generic model, designed to be applied in any manufacturing business that already possesses a stable manufacturing process and a deployment level in applying Lean tools. The failure of the application of the model outside does not demonstrate that the model is context specific but that in other to succeed its prerequisites should be observed. L&GBM was compatible with the structure of GKN Aerospace, Automotive Systems and Metals. The Kaizens in two out of three cases happened with the same level of enthusiasm and energy as in Brazil.

(Continued)

TABLE 3.3 (Continued)

L&GBM Response to Specialist's Inputs

Source of the Input	Main Questions	How L&GBM Is Addressing It?
Academia	19. How L&GBM maintain employee involvement after the Kaizen?	The difficulty here is that these three sites did not accomplish all prerequisites, especially regarding a leadership support, so they failed. Brazil, the model site, was able to accomplish all prerequisites, so it was able not only to do good Kaizens but also to demonstrate results
		As described in the prerequisites, L&GBM requires that the cell L&GBM will be applied to has already EI tools in place (operators already know and apply the most common EI tools, such as daily meeting, primary visual display, etc.); so, to keep the involvement, the model uses the already existing EI structure to keep the team enthusiasm and EI regarding the topic.
Academia	20. How L&GBM consider the evaluation of environmental changes?	The model presented in this project was applied in two circumstances—cell and value stream level.
		For the cell level, the model does not involve major changes in technology. Rather, the model focuses on behavioral and operations efficiency changes.
		For the second level flow, it may require major technology changes. This was not the case for the eight projects implemented due to the L&GBM implementation:
		Energy VS: (1) changing cold water pumping system; (2) energy reactive correction; (3) implementing of a system for monitoring and controlling compressed air leakages
		Metallic waste VS: (4) changing of cage design and VS
		Water/chemicals VS: (5) changing lubricant system;
		Oils VS: (6) implementing of internal oil regeneration system—with oil regeneration truck; (7) Implementing a system to reuse Cell 9 oil
		Waste VS: (8) implementing of automatic system for reuse of waste grease
		From the environmental perspective, major technological changes should be analyzed by adopting the LCA to avoid shifting the environmental burden

Source: Pampanelli, A., L&GBM, PhD Thesis, School of Engineering, UFRGS, Porto Alegre, Brazil, 2013.

specialists. Therefore, several inputs and questions were raised both by worldwide business/environmental specialists and academia. Now that the L&GBM and its results were already presented, this section is dedicated to reviewing and answering those inputs and a few others that came along the journey.

Table 3.3 highlights and answers the 20 key questions raised by both global specialists and academia regarding the L&GBM and its application.

4

Conclusions

Learning from the people who make history, for example, Charles Darwin, English naturalist, once said

> In the long history of humankind (and animal kind, too) those who learned to collaborate and improvise most effectively have prevailed.
> It is not the strongest of the species that survives, nor the most intelligent that survives. It is the one that is the most adaptable to change.

(Darwin, 2012).

In this sense, one of the main challenges faced by organizations involves building and maintaining a business in an ever-evolving market and entrepreneurial environment. As the social concerns about the environment grow, new systems and procedures must be incorporated into business operations. As a result, a new function has been integrated into the management function, namely, the environmental function (Darnalla et al., 2008; Nawrocka and Parkera, 2009).

This book has proposed a new model, the L&GBM, where the Green concern for environmental sustainability is integrated with Lean thinking. The model uses the Kaizen approach for addressing and improving mass and energy flows in a manufacturing environment that already possesses a specified Lean deployment level. The L&GBM was developed to investigate the potential benefits of integrating Green and Lean thinking for both the environment and businesses in terms of waste reduction, operational performance, and employee commitment.

L&GBM was created for integrating Lean thinking and Green thinking, merging the fundamental principles of Lean and Green to create a unique, integrated model. It introduces a new dimension into traditional Lean thinking, the environmental concerns, motivating a conceptual transition. Prior concepts, such as pure Lean and Green thinking, are the baggage. While integrating such concepts, L&GBM creates a new model derived from different sources, connecting fundamental blocks of a new way of thinking. As time passes, L&GBM seeks not only the integration of the social, environmental, and financial, but also equity, equitable value, importance, and priority for all its vectors, promoting connectedness within and outside the system.

L&GBM presents its own purpose: "Producing exactly what the customer wants, exactly when (with no delay), at fair price and minimum waste and environmental impact and the maximum productivity in the use of natural resources." L&GBM has also its own principles:

1. Identify a stable value stream (level 1, 2, or 3)
2. Identify in the flow of value the environmental aspects and impacts
3. Measure the value stream environmental impacts and the use of natural resources
4. Identify alternatives to
   a. Impact reduction
   b. Resources productivity in value stream
5. Pursue perfection—continuous improvement

As with other environmental practices, the L&GBM has the clear objective of improving the use of natural resources and reducing the environmental impact.

The idea of applying L&GBM is the integration with the continuous improvement process of a manufacturing value stream, where the Lean philosophy and ways of working are already in place. Following this, the subject of study of the L&GBM are the mass–energy flows of the manufacturing processes and the expected output from applying the model is the delivery of improvements in these thermodynamic flows (materials, chemicals, water, waste, effluent, and energy), contributing to the improvement of the overall performance. Because of this approach, L&GBM focuses on nontraditional sources of savings. Traditional Lean thinking considers only reductions in the seven classic Lean wastes (overproduction, waiting, transporting, inappropriate processing, unnecessary inventory, unnecessary/excess motion, and defects). With the introduction of environment concerns along the flow of value, other sources of waste can be targeted and reduced, thereby, maximizing overall savings. The L&GBM identifies and measures environmental aspects and impacts as well as the mass and energy inputs and outputs, while respecting the real flow of value based on the manufacturing value streams. Applying the L&GBM makes it easier to coordinate environmental and production performance metrics in a unique and integrated system. Also, it focuses on a simultaneous top-down and bottom-up approach for deploying continuous environmental improvements. All improvement opportunities that are identified by the L&GBM using the Kaizen approach are directly integrated into continuous improvement of the already existing structure due to Lean deployment. Prior to applying the proposed methodology, we identified seven prerequisites for implementing the L&GBM:

1. A stable process, with delivery achievement of over 90% (relevant to customer and business objectives)
2. A sufficient deployment level in terms of using and applying Lean tools
3. EI systems in place and mature
4. A supportive management team operating leadership standard work and Gemba leadership
5. Environmental awareness
6. Significant use of natural resources in the defined value stream
7. A structure for data collection

The model presented in this book was designed to be applied at the three levels of flow. Perhaps this book only presents results of its application to the cell level, which is the first-value stream level of a manufacturing business that supports the principles of Lean thinking and the second-level flow (i.e., the factory). This study can be expanded to the other value stream levels, including the third-level flow, or extended value stream level (i.e., multiple factories or the supply chain). These extensions will be the subject of future studies.

The model was tested in cells and second level of flow of a global manufacturing engineering company with different levels of Lean deployment and environmental impacts. The model used a cross-functional Kaizen team event to ensure that all team members were fully involved and had the opportunity to contribute their ideas. One of the clear gaps that were uncovered during the Kaizens was the lack of maturity and competence of the environmental organization within the company. This was due to a lack of front line focus on delivery and a gap in the understanding of the benefits of environmental deployment and an expectation that implementation was just driven by compliance. Combining a mature Lean system together with

Green thinking provides a conduit to deliver environmental step change and continuous-type improvements. It energizes the Lean team to search out further waste reductions by tapping into the technical expertise of the environmental team. For the environmental team, it provides a path and a process to deliver and sustain environmental improvements. Using the mature Lean system to "piggy back" environmental thinking can provide a quick fix to structural organizational deficiencies.

Summarizing the practical findings presented in this book, the following conclusions about the L&GBM can be presented, highlighting its contribution to practice:

- *L&GBM is a good pollution prevention strategy, reducing about 12% to 35% mass and energy flows*: L&GBM for a cell is able to reduce in average 35% the use of resources. For the sister cell case, the model is able to reduce 20%. In the value stream level, the model is able to reduce 12% the use of resources.
- *L&GBM can be used to reduce costs*: It is possible to reduce operational manufacturing mass and energy flow costs by about 2% to 8% (8% for cells, 2% for sister cells, and 4, 5% for the value stream level). In terms of direct cost savings, these four L&GBM improvement cycles produced alone a total of US$ 1.39M in savings. This result is four times higher than traditional Green practices (Cagno et al., 2005).
- *Confirmation of all prerequisites of L&GBM*: A variety of variables must be considered when applying the model. The pilot testing, the rollout of the model, and the application in other businesses outside Brazil confirmed the predicted prerequisites. The cells that fulfilled all prerequisites, including a sufficient deployment level in terms of applying Lean tools and a stable process, achieved better results. The prerequisites established are:
  1. Lean deployment level is critical
  2. Operational stability is a core requirement
  3. Leadership support is critical along all five steps of model development
  4. Top-down and bottom-up approach required for success
  5. Environmental awareness and use of resources is an important topic to prioritize where to start
  6. Data collection structure is key for deploying the model

- *L&GBM is data dependent*: As in many environmental practices, such as cleaner production, in the L&GBM, the data "tells the story," as the saying goes. Therefore, prework preparation and data collection are key steps in implementation and should be deployed properly to obtain good results during the Kaizen event. Brown et al. (2014) confirms this in a series of case studies in different sectors. Following the results of the application of the L&GBM for a cell in different manufacturing environments, a new prerequisite related to data collection was introduced in the L&GBM in order to manage what was found after the testing process.

- *L&GBM application for first and second levels of flow have different approaches*: For the first level of flow, L&GBM for a cell is more dependent on Lean (change agents) than environmental expertise. The improvement actions are simpler. L&GBM for a value stream environment requires a sharper focus. It requires a higher level of environmental understanding and competence in order to develop the analysis, the Kaizen, and set the action plan.

- *Traditional VSM thinking (divided by product families) is not applicable to the L&GBM*: For the value stream analysis, from an environmental perspective, it should be a site-based environmental impact and not just the impact of one value stream as there is a conjunction of environmental impacts that can create a system interference changing the overall impact; therefore, traditional VSM thinking (divided by product families) is not applicable because it will not consider the overall impact in the surroundings and the combination of environmental effects.

As discussed earlier, the model proposed here is different from other hybrid approaches and it is also distinct from pure Lean and/or pure Green practices, such as cleaner production and ecoefficiency, due to several characteristics.

The following theoretical conclusions can be generalized about the L&GBM, highlighting its contribution to knowledge:

- *L&GBM introduces a new dimension into traditional Lean thinking, the environmental concerns, motivating a conceptual transition.*
- *L&GBM fully integrates Lean thinking and Green thinking*, merging the fundamental principles of Lean and Green thinking to create a unique, integrated model.

- *L&GBM embraces a Lean-to-Green approach.* The implementation of the L&GBM should be a continuation of, or a second step to, continuous improvement where a Lean culture is already in place.
- *L&GBM focuses on nontraditional sources of savings.* Traditional Lean thinking considers only reductions in the seven classic Lean wastes. With the introduction of environmental concerns along the flow of value, other sources of waste can be targeted and reduced, maximizing overall savings.
- *L&GBM prioritizes manufacturing stability and customer focus.* It is called the Lean and Green business model because it is necessary to be Lean first.
- *L&GBM requires a sufficient level of manufacturing stability and Lean deployment prior to its introduction.* Other environmental practices, such as cleaner production and ecoefficiency, do not have this prerequisite.
- L&GBM identifies and measures environmental aspects and impacts as well as inputs and outputs, based on manufacturing value streams and the real flow of value. Neither cleaner production nor ecoefficiency focuses on manufacturing approaches to production and value streams to accomplish their objectives.
- *L&GBM focuses on a simultaneous top-down and bottom-up approach* for deploying continuous environmental improvements that are integrated into the continuous improvement structure of the existing Lean deployment.

Based on the results presented, the L&GBM shows that environmentally sustainable practices can be treated as an extension of Lean philosophy. Sustainability means "meeting the needs of current generations without compromising the ability of future generations to meet their needs in turn." The three fundamental impacts, social, environmental, and financial impacts (or people, planet, and profit) have evolved to redefine business objectives according to the original Brundtland philosophy (World Commission on Environment and Development, 1987). Thus, Lean thinking leads us toward sustainability initiatives. Because Lean thinking addresses economic sustainability, it is understood that the original concept can be expanded to achieve a much broader objective.

The U.S. Department of Commerce (2010) defines sustainable manufacturing as

> The creation of manufactured products that use processes that minimize negative environmental impacts, conserve energy and natural resources, are safe for employees, communities, and consumers and are economically sound.

Environmental sustainability, like Lean thinking, has a good track record of improving business finances because of the emphasis on eliminating waste. Extensive opportunities exist to save resources and money on the shop floor. This book applies the L&GBM using Kaizen exercises that draw on operators' and leaders' ideas and experience as well as appropriate Lean tools and techniques for identifying waste. This model can generate 8% in operational cost improvement. In a world of uncertainty concerning the economy and the environment, the L&GBM demonstrates a new and innovative approach to support the development of sustainable business.

5

Andrea's Real-Life Story behind the Research and the Book

> We cannot solve our problems with the same thinking we used when we created them

But in real life, how often do we try to solve the same problems using different reasoning, applying different lenses, trying to understand different paradigms, applying different ways of thinking? As a practicing environmental manager, I have tried and I know that we do really need to do much more to solve the problems facing manufacturing today than simply applying the same logic that we have always used.

This book tells a real-life story of research involving people from different corners of the world, a 250-year-old global multinational engineering corporation, two different universities, academics and industrialists, and much more. But overall, this is my story and the story of the many people that were with me on this journey. It is a story of open-minded people with hearts and souls that believe in creating new knowledge and new thinking, it is a story of breaking several paradigms. It is not one, but several stories in one and many ideas as part of many stories, many questions and some answers. And the story of my journey that I am inviting you to share.

THE BEGINNING...

I was introduced to Lean in 2006, but I was not originally a Lean person. My background is in chemical engineering, but I always had in my mind that my career should mean something, it should have a real purpose. That is how I became the "Green girl," in charge of the environmental engineering department of the subsidiary of a major British multinational automotive corporation based in Brazil. With more than 10 years of environmental management system in place at that time, the manufacturing units that I was responsible for were awarded and recognized several times for its environmental performance and consistent environmental improvement projects. So, the "Green girl."

I started working in GKN in 1999; it is a great company, with a genuine intention of developing people. I was very pleased with the work that I was doing and with the opportunities I had, but deep in my mind this was not enough. We had good environmental projects, good results, good ideas, but we could do more.

Following the deployment of Lean in 2004 into the factories, it quickly became apparent that the deployment of Lean process thinking needed to spread wider into the business and cover the nonmanufacturing functions like HR, finance, quality, procurement and sales as well; from this, a mirror Lean development programme was born and functional leaders were trained to deploy Lean through their functional responsibilities to all business processes.

For me, that moment was when I realized that Lean was something unusual and when corporate decided that all units over the world would be Lean, I was the one chosen by the board of directors of my site to receive Lean training overseas and to be a continuous improvement leader. I think that this was because of my curiosity and taste for constant learning, which my site directors recognized.

Most of the Lean knowledge I have today I learnt from my coauthor, Neil Trivedi. I met Neil in 2007 when I was training to be a continuous improvement leader. He was the person leading the training globally. I was a very good student. Even today we make fun of the thick Green notebook I had and the habit of copying every single word he said into it. I had also the habit of asking questions about what he had said, trying to understand the logic of this new subject that I was now learning.

I finished the training with one idea in my mind: The idea of doing more with less. The philosophy that I had been given the chance to study and practice so deeply for more than 8 months, which had made total sense to me and was wholly applicable to my Green world.

Einstein also stated: "Learn from yesterday, live for today, hope for tomorrow. The important thing is to never stop questioning".

So, this book was really started at the end of 2007.

I did well in the training and due to the results presented by my site, Neil decided to pilot test the training in Brazil by mirroring local training to the functional leaders.

That was an excellent opportunity for many reasons: first, I would have the chance to consolidate my Lean knowledge, review the subjects I had just learnt; second, the Brazil operation would have the opportunity to start creating its continuous improvement culture; and third, I would have Neil at the site three or four times that year and I could share with him my ideas of integrating Lean and Green.

So that was what happened.

My environmental team in Brazil and I started studying how we could integrate Lean and Green in a unique model that could be easily accepted by manufacturing.

I cannot proceed without highlighting one very special name: Fernando Dalvite, GKN Brazil environmental specialist, coordinator, and continuous improvement leader. He is the person behind most of the Kaizen implementation and testing that we did. Fernando, I, and some other colleagues put together the first version of what we called Lean and Green Kaizen. We conducted our first pilot on a Monobloc cell in October 2008. On this we discovered that, while the initiatives benefitted both the factory and the environment, there was no obvious link between the thinking process of environmental management and Lean systems.

When Neil came to Brazil for another flight of the training, I had the opportunity to share what we had done with him and to get his inputs to analyze our methods.

I don't remember the exact date, but I think it was in January 2009, when I was having a conference call with Neil to update him about Lean progress in Brazil and I mentioned to him

"I think this Lean and Green idea would make an excellent subject for a PhD."

And he answered:

"I do too. Why don't you go for it? I think this is very good idea!"

And I replied:

"No way! I think that it would be impossible to find a school and a supervisor that could accept me to study this topic."

And he said:

"Well, I know where you can study: Cardiff."

And I laughed:

"Me studying in UK??? Are you crazy?"

We ended that call.

Two weeks later Neil called saying that he had already talked with people in Cardiff at the Lean Enterprise Research Centre (LERC). There were some people there that were starting to study Lean and Green and they were very keen to talk to me. He suggested that I should call and talk to the professor to explain what I had done so far. If the expert liked me, I would have a good chance to be accepted there.

So that is what I did. In February 2009, I called LERC and shared my work; they were very interested, not only in the pilot and the Lean and Green Kaizen Model that I had put together but also because I was a Lean person with environmental expertise.

2009 was a very long year after that call.

The first challenge I had was to write a PhD project proposal: the longest five pages of my life. I had to write, in English, not in my native language, Portuguese, the background of my research, the ways of working, probable research question I would be interested in answering, and the timeline. I almost gave up. I had no idea what I was doing. But I did it and Neil helped again. I sent the paper to LERC and they liked it. I had experts interested in my work and a "go-ahead" from the university.

Writing five pages about my future research was, in fact, the easiest challenge I had that year. Some practical questions needed to be answered:

- Who will pay for the studies abroad? GKN?
- Will I move to United Kingdom?
- Can I keep my job?

Neil worked on sponsorship, but if I moved to United Kingdom I could not keep my job. So, how I would solve this?

That is when UFRGS Engineering School and Professor Andrea Bernardes became part of this journey. UFRGS is a federal university and one of the best in Brazil. I did all my studies there, 11 years of basic education at Colégio de Aplicação, 5 years of engineering school, environmental specialization degree, and master degree. Andrea had not been my professor then but, after an introduction from a friend, I went to talk to her in

May 2009. Andrea is an engineer with a PhD from Germany and great environmental expertise. I explained my project to her and the reasons why I could not study in Cardiff but I would have support from them and she accepted to supervise me.

But it was not so easy. I had to apply at UFRGS Engineering Scholl to be a PhD student. Application was in July and I had to hurry. Everything I had done in English and sent to Cardiff, I had to do it again, but now in Portuguese.

Accepted at UFRGS, PhD classes started in September 2009.

As Einstein once said: "No problem can be solved with the same level of consciousness that created it."

And you ask: "What about Cardiff?" After the acceptation at UFRGS, I had to apply at Cardiff Business School, LERC, Lean Enterprise Research Centre, to be a "visiting PhD student."

And that is what I did. January 2010, in a very cold winter in the United Kingdom, I arrived in Cardiff to start to write another chapter of this story in my life.

Couple of years after the PhD was started I asked Neil why he had supported me since the beginning and then he said: "When you proposed the PhD in Lean and Green it came as a natural opportunity to develop the concept in an industrial setting to provide cost reduction for GKN and benefits for the environment."

And then I thought, "Albert Einstein, I think I am starting to get your point."

YEAR ONE

I arrived in Cardiff on January 3, 2010. It was not my first time in the United Kingdom, but I will never forget that feeling and the excitement for starting such a unique journey in my life.

Neil met me at Heathrow and drove me directly to a hotel that became my home for the entire month and for all the other 15 weeks I visited Cardiff University in the three and a half years of my PhD (October 2010, March 2011, July 2011, June 2012, December 2012).

It was a very cold winter that year. BBC Weather was continuously announcing the dangers of something, unique to me, called "Frozen

Britain." "Don't take the trains, don't go outside and don't leave home if you don't need to." Home for me was room 420. It was a beautiful sight, from my hotel window, to see the Cardiff Millennium Centre, the home of Welsh rugby and Welsh dreams of glory, all covered in white snow. From someone coming from a tropical hot summer, what other dreams I would have?

One day dreaming about the rugby games, I questioned myself: How many matches I will need to play to succeed in this tournament? How many papers will I need to read? How many books? Do I have enough knowledge to digest all the information I am learning here?

In Cardiff, in the days that Britain was not frozen, I used to visit the university and city libraries, Cardiff City Centre, and the bookstores located at the university campus every day. Desperate and anxious with what I was going through, I got some books to try to answer these questions: *How to Get a PhD* by Estelle Phillips and Derek Pugh and *Guide to Publishing Scientific Papers* by Ann Korner.

I love books but, in that situation, they were not enough to explain the beauty and complexity of what I was experiencing. I had to feel that experience with all my senses and then let it go. I had to understand the academic side of Lean and the steps of a research project. But I did know that a certain Lean Lady was going to join me on the journey.

I got back home after being away from my husband and my dog for a month and I had learned some lessons:

- Studying in a university abroad was a dream that was becoming a reality.
- Welsh cakes are delicious and, with tea, they make a perfect combination.
- Cold weather is good, snow is beautiful but 'Frozen Britain' never again.
- I was not sure yet what my research questions were, and I had to find a way to do that.
- Although, from a business perspective, my idea of integrating Lean and Green made total sense, some academics doubted that this would make a PhD with a real contribution to practice and knowledge.
- Doing a PhD with a full-time job at GKN would be my Everest, my Stonehenge.

In order to overcome the barriers and decompose my Stonehenge, I started studying the fundamental building blocks of operations management,

Lean thinking, sustainability, and Green thinking very deeply. I was not sure about my research questions yet but definitely I had a start. I had to find at least some answers to some questions. I had to start by understanding the puzzle. And that is what I did.

YEAR TWO

To continue my story, I met, whom I kindly refer to as, the Lean Lady in October 2010, during my second visit to Cardiff. Dr. Pauline Found was, at that time, a Lean researcher and expert on sustainability. She was also an author. She had published the book *Staying Lean, Thriving, not Just Surviving*. And she was the professor chosen to be my PhD cosupervisor. When had I imagined deep in my mind that I would have a real author as supervisor, helping me with my research?

Pauline helped me a lot, not only in the research itself but also with real-life issues during this journey. And that is why she will always be the Lean Lady to me. Pauline made me understand the mental model I should follow to put together my research questions. She explained to me what "contribution to knowledge" really means. During my PhD, she introduced me to many people, made me show my work to many people, and let these people criticize my work in order to improve it. She also showed me how to get the train to go from Cardiff to any place in the United Kingdom and how to make real British tea. She advised me to always have a very small umbrella because in Cardiff the weather could change very quickly. She took me to an international conference of the Production and Operations Management Society (POMS) in the United States, in 2011. She introduced me to the real people that influenced my research. Because of her, John Bicheno, Doc Hall, Wallace Hopp, and Nick Rich are not just people that I read and believed in their ideas, but are people that I really met. They know me and I know them. Because of her, I heard several times from these people during the PhD: "Andrea, I know your work, Pauline told me about what you are doing and I think this is very good." To some extent, Pauline showed me that in the world of ideas, the distances are really very small and I was invited to be part of that world.

So in the end of 2010, with the support from Neil, Pauline, Andrea, Fernando, and my manager in Brazil, Leonidas Coutinho, PhD, got momentum and the L&GBM started to get shape.

We were able to pilot test the cell model twice in 2010, once in Brazil and then in the United Kingdom. With that experience, we were able to improve what we had and expand the ideas, applying the same cell model more than ten times in 2011, twice in the United States and several other times in the cells of GKN Brazilian operations in Porto Alegre and Charqueadas. The Kaizens we did that year alone saved around US$ 419,645.00, which represented a 5.5% reduction of the mass and energy flows through the cells.

On April 4, 2012, with all the testing and research I had done so far, I took the PhD qualifying examination at UFRGS. At this point, the L&GBM was born. Although there was no doubt about the practical, environmental, and financial results of the model, there was still some skepticism from the examiners regarding the model itself. Was there something unique that would represent a real contribution to knowledge and science?

In other words, to have my PhD I had to find a way to explain how the integration of two different ways of thinking, Lean thinking and Green thinking, with its own characteristics, boundaries and languages would create a new and unique approach. And that was no easy task.

I got back to Cardiff again in July 2011 and June 2012 with just one thing in mind: I had to solve that equation. At that point in my research I had to be able to explain why my work was something different. Pauline shared my 138-page qualification report with several experts and academics that made me defend the questions in order to find the answers I needed.

At that point, Cardiff was already my second home and the United Kingdom was not a mystery anymore. I loved it all and I felt myself already part of that environment. With that feeling inside of me, being able to understand a different way of being, totally different of what I was used to and from where I came from, it was easier for me to cross the boundaries that separate Lean from Green. It was clear to me that I had to explain Lean to Green and vice versa.

I have no doubt today that I would not have the same result in my research if I was not living in that constant exposure to the different ideas and challenges during the PhD. Going backward and forward to Cardiff so many times during this journey showed me this. Cardiff made me experience in life what I was creating as research. When I understood that, L&GBM became a real model, integrated, clear, and unique, that would make sense to both environmental managers and Lean experts.

YEAR THREE: THE END

While in Cardiff, I had the academic environment to help develop the research, back home in Brazil, and I had the industrial playground to apply the ideas.

This research would never, ever have happened without the support I received from GKN. I am not saying that just because they paid for the studies abroad. They did much more than that. GKN in Brazil was open to pilot, test, and rollout my ideas, developing more than 30 cell Kaizens during the PhD period and also applying the model for the second level of flow—the value stream. I had a train full of people on board, more than 350.

My two managers during this period, Leonidas Coutinho and Jader Hilzendeger, also guaranteed me one day a week off work to focus on my research and my PhD. Working and studying at the same time, I would never have been able to finish my research in those three and a half years without the support I received from them. Of course I had support at home too. My husband and my dog were my true source of love and energy to transform ideas into reality.

With a heart and soul full of good inspirations and feelings, L&GBM also proved to be a very good business opportunity. In terms of direct cost savings, L&GBM application produced a total of US$ 1.39 million in savings.

In the end of the journey, in December 2012, I sent Doc Hall the whole research to get his input on the work that I was developing. I had met Doc in July 2011, during the LERC Annual Conference, when he presented his book *Compression*, and I had a chance to share with him my research. At the end of the conference, when he was able to understand my Kaizens and what I was doing, he came to me and said, "I like what you have done and how you are doing it. Having a finite environment is a good way to start and I think you are doing it right. Please let me know about your progress. I would be interested in knowing how you are deploying your ideas."

So in the end of 2012, when the work was almost completed, I sent Doc my work and several questions. And he sent back to me, not only the words of a genius, a person that is able to see more deeply and further than many others, but also the go ahead I needed to finalize my work. Some of what he said was

Two phrases emerging attract people to Compression Thinking: 'Do better using much less,' or 'Live better using much less.' These suggest that using far fewer resources helps assure a more sustainable planet on which we may enjoy life a bit, and not just struggle to survive. This sets a goal, which is necessary to motivate action, but devoid (entirely lacking or free from) of content. A guide to taking action requires a more extensive model because we are trying to change habits of thought, and that requires knowledge as well as motivation. Dealing with this, one is soon back to dealing with preconceptions. I think your L&GBM is model to motivate conceptual transition. Prior concepts are baggage, some of which must be left behind to get on a train moving down a different track, and some of which can be moved to the new train. This learning process takes time.

With that in mind, I finalized my research.

On August 26, 2013, I defended my PhD thesis at UFRGS with Neil and Pauline participating actively by videoconference. The journey I started in 2009 was ending. I received from examiners a very prestigious title; the research was awarded with the highest honors.

I was very pleased with the recognition but deep in my heart I started missing something. The PhD had changed my life and the new paradigms and ideas created by L&GBM had changed my thinking and way of working.

What about my journey? You know that feeling we have at the end of a vacation when we visited a wonderful place, where we learned a lot and were very happy; that special trip that we would remember throughout our life? That was my journey to the frontier where academia meets industry. I learned what I did not know. I explored what was not explored. I overcame my limits. When this happens, it is impossible to forget. Trying to understand the world, I discovered myself as a person. Trying to decodify the frontier I discovered my mind and spirit. I had climbed my Everest.

Beautiful view, full heart, inexplicable feeling—I hope you have enjoyed reading my journey.

Glossary of Terms

Cleaner production: Cleaner production is a preventive, company-specific environmental protection initiative. It is intended to minimize waste and emissions and maximize product output.

Eco-design and design for environment (DFE): This is based on the principle of designing physical objects and services to comply with the principles of economic, social, and ecological sustainability in all stages of product or service development with the ultimate goal of reducing environmental impact in the whole product or service life cycle.

Eco-effectiveness: This is based on a cradle-to-cradle or closed-loop design strategy reflecting natural systems. These are not necessarily efficient individually, but are effective since there is no waste in the natural system as a whole.

Eco-efficiency: The concept of eco-efficiency was introduced by the World Business Council for Sustainable Development (WBCSD) (2000). It is based on creating more while using fewer resources and creating less waste and pollution.

Employee involvement: Kaizen relies on ongoing effort and engagement of people—it is based on the constant effort for involving and integrating people, from shop-floor workers to senior executives.

Environmental management systems (EMS): An EMS is a structured framework for managing an organization's significant environmental impacts. The standard for EMS is ISO 14001, which is based on Deming's cycle of plan, do, check, and act.

Environmental performance evaluation (EPE): EPE is a management technique that allows evaluation of a company's environmental performance through self-defined criteria and requirements.

Industrial ecology (IE): A framework for thinking about and organizing human economic and social systems in ways that resemble natural ecosystems.

Industrial symbiosis (IS): This demands resolute attention to the flow of materials and energy via local and regional economies. IS engages traditionally separate industries in a collective approach to competitive advantage involving physical exchange of materials, energy, water, and/or by-products.

Kaizen: Smaller steps of improvement, often suggested by the people working on a line or cell (as opposed to management or the improvement team).

Lean: A strategy for doing business efficiently, with the workforce involved in making improvements continuously, making exactly what the customer wants when they want it (and not before), and minimizing wastes of all kinds.

Life cycle analysis (LCA): LCA models the complex interaction between a product and the environment from cradle to grave. Life cycle analysis can be an expensive and lengthy process but provides in-depth data on the environmental impacts.

Natural capitalism: This concept pictures a new industrial system based on very different mindset and values from conventional capitalism. Natural capital refers to the natural resources and ecosystem services that make economic activities possible.

Pollution prevention: Pollution is prevented at source rather than emissions being treated at the end of the pipe.

Sustainability: A systemic concept relating to the continuity of economic, social, and environmental aspects of human society.

The biosphere rule: This is the mantra for environmentally responsible materials management: "reduce, reuse, and recycle" is not as Lean as it seems.

The natural step (TNS): TNS framework's definition of sustainability includes four system conditions (scientific principles) required for a sustainable world.

Triple bottom line (TBL): The TBL agenda aims to integrate into corporate strategy and corporate governance a focus not only on the economic value that they add, but also on the environmental and social value that they add—or destroy.

Value stream mapping: This process refers to identifying families of products, then for each family identifying each step in their manufacturing process and highlighting which steps are not adding value.

References

Baas, L. 2007. To make zero emissions technologies and strategies become a reality, the lessons learned of cleaner production dissemination have to be known. *Journal of Cleaner Production* 15: 1205–16.

Berger, A. 1997. Continuous improvement and kaizen: Standardization and organizational designs. *Integrated Manufacturing Systems* 8: 110–17.

Bhasin, S. and P. Burcher. 2006. Lean viewed as a philosophy. *Journal of Manufacturing Technology Management* 17: 56–72.

Bicheno, J. 2000. *The Lean Toolbox*, 2nd ed. Buckingham, U.K.: PICSIE Books.

Biggs, C. 2009. Exploration of the integration of Lean and environmental improvement. PhD Thesis, Cranfield University, Cranfield, U.K.

Boons, F., W. Spekkink, and Y. Mouzakitis. 2011. The dynamics of industrial symbiosis: A proposal for a conceptual framework based upon a comprehensive literature review. *Journal of Cleaner Production* 19: 905–91.

Boyle, C. 1999. Cleaner production workshops. *Journal of Cleaner Production* 7: 83–7.

Brown, A., J. Amundsen, and F. Badurden. 2014. Sustainable value stream mapping (Sus-VSM) in different manufacturing system configurations: Application case studies. *Journal of Cleaner Production* 85: 164–79.

Burke, P. 2006. *Hibridismo Cultural*. São Leopoldo, Brazil: Unisinos.

Cagno, E., P. Trucco, and L. Tardini. 2005. Cleaner production and profitability: Analysis of 134 industrial pollution prevention (P2) project reports. *Journal of Cleaner Production* 13: 593–605.

Calia, R., F. Guerrini, and R. Castro. 2009. The impact of six sigma in the performance of a pollution prevention program. *Journal of Cleaner Production* 17: 1303–10.

Capra, F. 1996. *A Teia da Vida "The web of life"* (Translation of Newton Roberval Eichemberg). São Paulo, Brazil: Cultrix.

Carson, R. 2010. *Primavera silenciosa* (Translation of Claudia Sant'Ana Martins). São Paulo, Brazil: Gaia.

Cobert, C. and R. Klassen. 2006. Extending the horizons: Environmental excellence as key to improving operations. *Manufacturing and Service Operations Management* 8: 5–22.

Darnalla, N., I. Henriquest, and P. Sadorskyb. 2008. Do environmental management systems improve business performance in an international setting? *Journal of International Management* 14: 364–76.

Darwin, C. 2012. IZ quotes. Available at: http://izquotes.com/author/charles-darwin (accessed December 17, 2012).

Diaz-Elsayad, N., A. Jondral, S. Greinacher, D. Dornfeld, and G. Lanza. 2013. Assessment of lean and green strategies by simulation of manufacturing systems in discrete production environments. *CIRP Annals—Manufacturing Technology* 62: 475–8.

Diehl, J. and H. Brezet. 2004. Design for sustainability: An approach for international development, transference and local implementation. In *International Conference on Environmental Management for Sustainable Universities—EMSU 2004, Proceedings*, 3rd edn, 2004, Colonia Tecnológico Monterrey, Monterrey, Mexico.

Dieleman, H. and D. Huisingh. 2006. Games by which to learn and teach about sustainable development: Exploring the relevance of games and experiential learning for sustainability. *Journal of Cleaner Production* 14: 837–47.

Dues, C., K. Tan, and M. Lim. 2012. Green as the new Lean: How to use Lean practices as a catalyst to greening your supply chain. *Journal of Cleaner Production* 1: 1–8.

Florida, R. 1996. Lean and Green: The move to environmentally conscious manufacturing. *California Business Review* 39: 80–105.

Found, P. 2009. Lean and low environmental impact manufacturing. In *POMS 2009— 20th Annual Conference of the Production and Operations Management Society, 2009, Proceedings of POM 2009*, Production and Operations Management Society, Orlando, FL, pp. 126–30.

Fresner, J. 1998. Starting continuous improvement with a cleaner production assessment in an Austrian textile mill. *Journal of Cleaner Production* 6: 85–91.

Galeazzo, A., A. Furlan, and A. Vinelli. 2014. Lean and green in action: Interdependencies and performance of pollution prevention projects. *Journal of Cleaner Production* 85: 191–200.

Gavronski, I., R. Klassen, S. Vachon, and L. Nascimento. 2012. A learning and knowledge approach to sustainable operations. *International Journal of Production Economics* 140: 183–92.

Gavronski, I., E. Paiva, R. Teixeira, and M. Andrade. 2013. ISO 14001 certified plants in Brazil—Taxonomy and practices. *Journal of Cleaner Production* 39: 32–41.

Glavic, P. and R. Lukman. 2007. Review of sustainability terms and their definitions. *Journal of Cleaner Production* 15: 1875–85.

Gordon, P. 2001. *Lean and Green: Profit for your workplace and environment*. San Francisco, CA: Berrett-Koehler Publishers.

Gustashaw, D. and R. Hall. 2008. From Lean to Green: Interface, Inc. *Association for Manufacturing Excellence's Target Magazine* 24: 6–14.

Haes, H. 1993. Applications of life cycle assessment: Expectations, drawbacks and perspectives. *Journal of Cleaner Production* 1: 131–7.

Hajmohammad, S., S. Vachon, R. Klassen, and I. Gavronski. 2013. Lean Management and supply chain management: Their role in green practices and performance. *Journal of Cleaner Production* 39: 312–20.

Hall, R. 2010. *Compression: Meeting the Challenges of Sustainability through Vigorous Learning Enterprises*. Boca Raton, FL: CRC Press.

Hall, R. 2011. Compression thinking. In *LERC Annual Conference 2011, Proceedings*, 10th edn, Cardiff University, Cardiff, U.K., pp. 13–28.

Hawken, P., A. Lovins, and H. Lovins. 1999. *Natural Capitalism: Creating the New Industrial Revolution*. Boston, MA: Little Brown & Company.

Hines, P., M. Holweg, and N. Rich. 2004. Learning to evolve: A review of contemporary lean thinking. *International Journal of Operations & Production Management* 24: 994–1011.

Hopp, W. and M. Spearman. 2008. *Factory Physics*, International Edition. New York: McGraw-Hill.

International Organization for Standardization (ISO). 2004. ISO 14001: Environmental management systems—Requirements with guidance for use. ISO, Geneva, Switzerland.

Jabbour, C., E. Silva, E. Paiva, and F. Santos. 2012. Environmental management in Brazil: Is it a completely competitive priority ? *Journal of Cleaner Production* 21: 11–22.

Jasch, C. 2000. Environmental performance evaluation and indicators. *Journal of Cleaner Production* 8: 79–88.

Karim, A. and K. Zaman. 2013. A methodology for effective implementation of lean strategies and its performance evaluation in manufacturing organizations. *Business Process Management* 19: 169–96.

King, A. A. and M. J. Lenox. 2001. Lean and Green? An empirical examination of the relationship between lean production and environmental performance. *Production and Operations Management* 10: 244–56.

Kiperstock, A. 2000. Implementation of cleaner production practices with the support of a diploma course. *Journal of Cleaner Production* 8: 375–9.

Korhone, J. 2007. 'From Material Flow Analysis to Material Flow Management': Strategic sustainability management on a principle level. *Journal of Cleaner Production* 15: 1585–95.

Kurdve, M., K. Romvall, M. Bellgran, and E. Torstensson. 2011. A systematic approach for identifying lean and green improvements related to packaging material in assembly. In *Swedish Production Symposium, SPS11, 2011—Proceedings of SPS11*, Lund University, Lund, Sweden.

Lenzen, M. 2008. Sustainable island businesses: A case study of Norfolk Island. *Journal of Cleaner Production* 16: 2018–35.

Lozano, R. 2008. Envisioning sustainability three-dimensionally. *Journal of Cleaner Production* 16: 1838–46.

Lozano, R. 2012. Towards a better understanding of sustainability into companies' systems: An analysis of voluntary corporate initiatives. *Journal of Cleaner Production* 25: 14–26.

Maxwell, J., S. Rothenberg, and B. Schenck. 1993. Does Lean mean Green? The implications of Lean production for the environmental management. International Motor Vehicle Program, MIT, Cambridge, MA.

Mazur, L. and L. Miles. 2010. *Conversa com os mestres da sustentabilidade*. São Paulo, Brazil: Gente.

Meadows, D. H., D. L. Meadows, J. Randers, and W. Behrens. 1972. *The Limits to Growth*. New York: Universe Books.

Moraes, C., A. Kieling, M. Caetano, and L. Gomes. 2010. Life cycle analysis (LCA) for the incorporation of rice hush ash in mortar coating. *Resources, Conservation and Recycling* 54: 1170–6.

Moreira, F., A. Alves, and R. Sousa. 2010. Towards eco-efficient Lean production systems. *IFIP Advances in Information and Communication Technology* 322: 100–8.

Nawrocka, D., T. Brorson, and T. Lindhqvist. 2009. ISO 14001 in environmental supply chain practices. *Journal of Cleaner Production* 17: 1435–43.

Nawrocka, D. and T. Parkera. 2009. Finding the connection: Environmental management systems and environmental performance. *Journal of Cleaner Production* 17: 447–54.

Nielsen, S. 2007. What has modern ecosystem theory to offer to cleaner production, industrial ecology and society? The views of an ecologist. *Journal of Cleaner Production* 15: 1639–53.

Ohno, T. 1988. *Toyota Production System: Beyond Large-Scale Production*. Portland, OR: Productivity Press.

Pampanelli, A. 2013. L&GBM. PhD Thesis, School of Engineering, UFRGS.

Perron, G. M., R. P. Côte, and J. F. Duffy. 2006. Improving environmental awareness training in business. *Journal of Cleaner Production* 14: 551–62.

Pettersen, J. 2009. Defining lean production: Some conceptual and practical issues. *The Total Quality Management Journal* 21: 127–42.

Pollitt, D. 2006. Culture change makes Crusader fit for the future: Training in lean manufacturing helps to transform company. *Human Resource Management International Digest* 14: 11–4.

Porter, M. and C. van der Linde. 1995. Toward a new conception of environmental competitive relationship. *The Journal of Economic Perspectives* 9: 97–118.

Remmen, A. and B. Lorentzen. 2000. Employee participation and cleaner technology: Learning processes in environmental teams. *Journal of Cleaner Production* 8: 365–73.

Rich, N. 2006. Understanding the lean journey. In *Evolution of Lean: Lessons from the Workplace*, N. Rich, N. Bateman, A. Esain, L. Massey, and D. Samuel (Eds.), pp. 11–31. Cambridge, U.K.: Cambridge University Press.

Robèrt, K. H. 2002a. Strategic sustainable development: Selection, design and synergies of applied tools. *Journal of Cleaner Production* 10: 197–214.

Robèrt, K. H. 2002b. *The Natural Step Story. Seeding a Quiet Revolution*. Gabriola Island, BC: New Society Publishers.

Rondinelli, D. and G. Vastag. 2000. Panacea, common sense, or just a label: The value of ISO 14001 environmental management systems. *European Management Journal* 18: 499–510.

Rothenberg, S. 2001. Lean, Green and the quest for superior environmental performance. *Production and Operations Management* 10: 228–43.

Rother, M. and J. Shook. 2003. *Learning to See*. Cambridge, MA: Lean Enterprise Institute.

Salleh, N. A. M., S. Kasolang, and A. Jaffar. 2012. Green lean total quality information management in Malaysian automotive companies. *Procedia Engineering* 41: 1708–13.

Saurin, T. and C. Ferreira. 2009. The impact of lean working conditions: A case study of a harvester assembly line in Brazil. *International Journal of Industrial Ergonomics* 39: 403–12.

Schrettle, S., A. Hinz, M. Scherrer-Rathje, and T. Friedli. 2014. Turning sustainability into action: Explaining firms' sustainability efforts and their impact in performance. *International Journal of Production Economics* 147 (Part A): 73–84.

Slack, N., S. Chambers, and R. Johnston. 2004. *Operations Management*. London, U.K.: Prentice Hall.

Stern, N. 2007. *The Economics of Climate Change: The Stern Review*. Cambridge, U.K.: Cambridge University Press.

Stone, L. 2000. When case studies are not enough: The influence of corporate culture and employee attitudes on the success of cleaner production initiatives. *Journal of Cleaner Production* 8: 353–9.

Tanimoto, A., A. Kiperstok, and D. Fontana et al. 2008. O Papel da universidade na introdução de práticas de Produção Limpa na Bahia: A UFBA e a Rede TECLIM. In *Prata da casa: Construindo Produção Limpa na Bahia*, A. Kiperstok (Ed.), pp. 19–42. Santa Bárbara, CA: Salvador.

Tibbs, H. 1992. Industrial ecology: An environmental agenda for industry. *Whole Earth Review* 77: 4–19.

US Department of Commerce. International Trade Administration. 2010. How does commerce define sustainable manufacturing? Available at: http://www.trade.gov/competitiveness/sustainablemanufacturing/how_doc_defines_SM.asp (accessed January 20, 2014).

US Environmental Protection Agency (EPA). 2006. The Lean and environment toolkit. Available at: www.epa.gov/Lean (accessed December 17, 2012).

Vais, A., V. Miron, M. Pedersen, and J. Folke. 2006. Lean and Green at a Romanian secondary tissue paper and board mill—putting theory into practice. *Resources, Conservation and Recycling* 46: 44–74.

Venselaar, J. 1995. Environmental training: Industrial needs. *Journal of Cleaner Production* 3: 9–12.

Verrier, B., B. Rose, E. Caillaud, and H. Remita. 2014. Combining organizational performance with sustainable development issues: The Lean and green project benchmarking repository. *Journal of Cleaner Production* 85: 83–93.

Womack, J. and D. Jones. 1996. *Lean Thinking*. New York: Free Press.

Womack, J., D. Jones, and D. Ross. 1990. *The Machine that Changed the World*. New York: Free Press.

World Business Council for Sustainable Development. 2000. *Ecoefficiency: Creating More Value with Less Impact*. Geneva, Switzerland: WBCSD.

World Commission on Environment and Development. 1987. *Our Common Future*. Oxford, U.K.: Oxford University Press. Available at: http://www.un-documents.net/wced-ocf.htm (accessed December 17, 2012).

Yang, M., P. Hong, and S. Modi. 2011. Impact of lean manufacturing and environmental management on business performance: An empirical study of manufacturing firms. *International Journal of Production Economics* 129: 251–61.

Zokaei, K., F. Martinez, and D. Vazquez et al. 2010. Best practice tools and techniques for carbon reduction and climate change: Lean and Green Report. Lean Enterprise Research Centre, Cardiff University, Cardiff, U.K.

Authors

Dr. Andrea Pampanelli has more than 15 years of environmental and 5 years of Lean experience working for GKN Driveline.

During her career in GKN, Andrea developed more than 100 EHS and Lean research projects applied to GKN in partnership with Brazilian local universities and won more than 15 excellence awards from GKN Driveline, GKN Group, and OEM customers.

She has a bachelor's degree in chemical engineering, an MBA in environmental management, and a master's degree in production engineering from Federal University of Rio Grande do Sul (UFRGS) in Brazil, and a specialization degree in safety engineering by Unisinos in Brazil.

Andrea started her Lean and Green PhD project in 2010. Developed in partnership between UFRGS in Brazil and LERC, Lean Enterprise Research Center, in Cardiff University in the United Kingdom, Andrea was supervised by Dr. Andrea Bernardes at UFRGS and co-supervised by Dr. Pauline Found at LERC.

The Lean and Green business model developed during her PhD was applied and pilot-tested in GKN operations in Brazil, the United States, and the United Kingdom. Andrea finished her PhD with high honor in August, 2013, having published more than 10 academic papers during the period.

Today Dr. Pampanelli works as regional environmental manager at GKN Driveline Americas.

Her research and PhD thesis were fundamental in the development of this book.

Neil Trivedi is a highly experienced strategy and transformation consultant and qualified Lean expert, with broad experience across global platforms within the automotive, aerospace, food, FMCG, transportation, biomedical, and public sectors. He has been instrumental in helping organizations improve their performance by collaboratively tackling complex business problems and in designing and implementing solutions that demonstrate tangible benefits to businesses.

Neil previously worked for GKN as the Global Business Process Excellence Director, where he deployed Lean across all levels into manufacturing and business processes. Prior to this, he worked at Mars and Royal Mail in a variety of operational management roles deploying Lean across Europe in supply chain, production, project management, and quality.

He was educated at Leeds University, Imperial College London, and Cardiff University. He holds a BSc (Hons), an MBA, and an MSc (distinction).

Dr. Pauline Found is a senior lecturer in Lean operations management at University of Buckingham.

She was previously senior research fellow of the Lean Enterprise Research Centre (LERC) at Cardiff University, where she worked for 9 years and was involved in a range of research, knowledge transfer, and engaging in projects and executive education, as well as writing books and papers on Lean. She is coauthor of *Staying Lean: Thriving Not Just Surviving*, for which she holds a Shingo Research and Professional Publication Prize (2009).

Pauline previously worked for Imperial Tobacco and BP, in a range of research, project planning, and senior management roles, including IT, purchasing, operations planning, HR, and quality.

Dr. Found was educated at The Open University, Cardiff University, and Bristol University. She is a fellow of the Institute of Operations Management (FIOM) and a member of the Chartered Institute of Purchasing and Supply (MCIPS) and the American Society of Quality (ASQ). She holds a PhD, an MBA, a BSc (Hons), a BA, and a PG diploma in environmental management. She was president of the International POMS (Production and Operations Management Society) College of Behavior 2009–2011.

Index